C000226169

# Praise for
# *Smart Big Moves*

'An unusual book on business strategy. We all know the story about profitable growth, increased returns and BHAG's [big hairy audacious goals] driving growth. The relieving fact in this book by Strebel and Ohlsson is its smart way of telling a story that "we" so easily forget – the story about our egos and their influence on business results. Read this book – to remain a little smarter.'

*Sten Scheibye, President and CEO, Coloplast A/S*

'This is a different kind of business book: it combines a great story with great business insight to make strategic shifts work for your business. I love this book!'

*Mr Karimattam Davasia, President and Executive Director,*
*Mahindra & Mahindra Ltd*

'Large companies with household names fail and disappear from the corporate landscape. Others reinvent themselves in their moments of crisis. Will we learn from the smart and stupid moves of others? This book shows us how to use smart psychology, strategy and risk management to turn strategic shifts into winners. Read it!'

*Renato Fassbind, CFO, Credit Suisse*

'Strebel and Ohlsson have written a highly recommendable short guide to great strategy. It combines business logic with psychological insight, using smart psychology, strategy and risk management for successful growth.'

*Michael F. Bigham, Partner, Abingworth Management*

# SMART
# BIG
# MOVES

FT Prentice Hall
FINANCIAL TIMES

In an increasingly competitive world, we believe it's quality of thinking that gives you the edge – an idea that opens new doors, a technique that solves a problem or an insight that simply makes sense of it all. The more you know, the smarter and faster you can go.

That's why we work with the best minds in business and finance to bring cutting-edge thinking and best learning practice to a global market.

Under a range of leading imprints, including *Financial Times Prentice Hall*, we create world-class print publications and electronic products bringing our readers knowledge, skills and understanding, which can be applied whether studying or at work.

To find out more about Pearson Education publications or tell us about the books you'd like to find, you can visit us at **www.pearsoned.co.uk**

PEARSON
Education

# SMART
# BIG
# MOVES

## THE STORY BEHIND STRATEGIC BREAKTHROUGHS

### PAUL STREBEL
### ANNE-VALÉRIE OHLSSON

**FT** Prentice Hall
FINANCIAL TIMES

*An imprint of* **Pearson Education**
Harlow, England • London • New York • Boston • San Francisco • Toronto
Sydney • Tokyo • Singapore • Hong Kong • Seoul • Taipei • New Delhi
Cape Town • Madrid • Mexico City • Amsterdam • Munich • Paris • Milan

**PEARSON EDUCATION LIMITED**

Edinburgh Gate
Harlow CM20 2JE
Tel: +44 (0)1279 623623
Fax: +44 (0)1279 431059
Website: www.pearsoned.co.uk

First published in Great Britain in 2008

© Pearson Education 2008

The rights of Paul Strebel and Anne-Valérie Ohlsson to be identified as authors of this work have been asserted by them in accordance with the Copyright, Designs and Patents Act 1988.

ISBN: 978-0-273-71426-2

*British Library Cataloguing-in-Publication Data*
A catalogue record for this book is available from the British Library

*Library of Congress Cataloging-in-Publication Data*
Strebel, Paul.
    Smart big moves : the story behind strategic breakthroughs / Paul Strebel and Anne-Valérie Ohlsson.
        p. cm.
    Includes bibliographical references and index.
    ISBN 978-0-273-71426-2
    1. Organizational change. 2. Strategic planning. 3. Corporate reorganizations. I. Ohlsson, Anne-Valérie. II. Title.
    HD58.8.S773 2008
    658.4'012--dc22
                                    2008016405

We are grateful for permission to reproduce the screenshot on page 47 © Copyright Organic Monitor.

10 9 8 7 6 5 4 3 2
12  11  10  09

Typeset in 10.5/14pt Minion by 30
Printed in Great Britain by Henry Ling Limited, at the Dorset Press, Dorchester, DT1 1HD

*The publisher's policy is to use paper manufactured from sustainable forests.*

# Contents

# Acknowledgements

For the past 15 years, we have been studying what drives strategic breakthroughs. We first looked at the impact of industry breakpoints and found that, while external forces are important from time to time, the more frequent breakthroughs come from big strategic moves that managers make to trigger the further development of a business. The keys to breakthroughs are to be found mainly inside the company, even inside management heads, rather than outside. These early findings were discussed with the hundreds of managers who attended the IMD's Breakthrough Programme for Senior Executives in the early 2000s and the Programme for Executive Development more recently. We are indebted to the participants on these and other IMD programmes for the spirit in which they shared their related experience and points of view – in particular, the drivers of their decision making.

Bjorn Oste gracefully allowed us to use his personal history and the real-life Oatly company as the basis for the story in this book. Fortunately, the reality of Oatly is much less tumultuous than the story about 'Oaty' makes it out to be for the purposes of illustration. We wish him and the company continuing success.

We would like to thank IMD's president, Peter Lorange, for his support of this research and Pierre Landolt, CEO of the Sandoz Family Foundation, for the donation to IMD that supports the post of chair held by one of us. We also thank Liz Gooster, of FT Prentice Hall, for insightful suggestions, editorial improvements and support.

Books are not nine-to-five projects that one can leave behind at the end of the day. We are grateful to our families and friends for their support and patience in dealing with the single-minded focus that goes with writing.

Lausanne, November 2007

# Introduction

Human beings have told stories since the dawn of time, using them to share values, beliefs and codes of conduct. They remain one of the most powerful means of sharing. When we considered writing this book, we wanted to talk about our findings in a way that would not be overly pedantic. We chose to write a story based on a real company, together with real-world case studies, and in this way provide the context for sharing the keys to success for shifts in strategy – what we call big moves, involving a large commitment of resources to a new goal. Big moves can make or break a company.

As an example of what we mean by a smart big move, consider the strategic breakthrough made by Wipro Ltd – the Indian company that originally was making vegetable oils and soaps.

When Wipro moved into the distribution of computer hardware in the early 1970s, most observers saw it as a wild big bet with very limited chances of success. However, Wipro already had an extensive distribution network, as well as a reputation for high-quality service and customer care, and the closed Indian market was clamouring for hardware after IBM withdrew from India. What looked like a big strategic bet was, in fact, a much surer move.

Later, when Wipro tried to develop customized software for its clients, it initially ran into problems because it had no software development experience. Yet, once it had acquired that know-how, it successfully launched and rolled out Wipro Technology to sell licensed software and computer services around the globe. What previously was a strategic shift with little chance of success had become a much surer move and, by 2000, approximately 80 per cent of the company's income came from its IT businesses and the majority of the company's revenues came from outside India –

in fact, 75 per cent came from companies based in California. (You'll find out more about the big moves made by Wipro in Chapter 1.)

In the late 1990s, ABB, the European engineering company, decided to 'transform itself from a traditional multinational industrial group into an agile knowledge-based company dependent on intellectual assets, rather than on heavy engineering assets'. Its Chairman, Percy Barnevik, and CEO, Göran Lindahl, divested the group's power-generation, railway equipment and nuclear power businesses and acquired software and automation systems companies. ABB went from being a heavy equipment supplier to employing more software engineers than Microsoft.

However, ABB, the product of many acquisitions, was highly fragmented. It had no common processes, more than 500 enterprise resource planning (ERP) systems and no real software systems experience. The customers it knew how to reach wanted products and equipment, not software solutions. How could Barnevik and Lindahl have made such a stupid big move, such a risky big bet?

We have to remember that the dotcom boom was in full swing and ABB had been named the 'most respected company of the year' for the fourth consecutive time. Barnevik and Lindahl fell into the psychological trap created by their hubris, which is presumptuous pride that invites disaster: they obviously believed that they could run any business and turn ABB into the darling of the dotcom era, which turned out to have disastrous consequences. (You'll find out more about the smart and stupid big moves and what happened to ABB in Chapter 5.)

Despite all that's been written about the virtues of slow-but-steady corporations, the Wipro and ABB examples illustrate that multinationals' growth and evolution are not only fuelled by continual adaptation but also by major strategic shifts – big moves involving a major commitment of resources to a new strategic goal. At key points – driven by managerial ambition, company dynamics or the business environment – companies make dramatic shifts. These are big moves typically involving a different set of products or services, a new customer base and/or new ways of operating. These big moves are not sudden events. While the decision to make a big move occurs at a point in time, the execution of the move takes time. If the move fails, it can threaten the company's performance – even its survival. It is those successful strategic shifts that we call strategic breakthroughs.

Looking at the history of companies, it soon becomes clear that you can't separate the world into smart and stupid companies. Even the most successful companies can make stupid big moves from which they have difficulty recovering. So, this book is not about smart and stupid companies – a company is only as smart as its last big move. It is about smart and stupid strategic shifts – that is, the difference between successful and unsuccessful, discontinuous changes in strategic direction. The challenge is to reduce the chances of a stupid big move and increase the number of smart ones. If not selected and managed properly, big moves are big bets with high chances of failure; properly selected and managed they are surer moves with much greater chances of becoming a breakthrough.

## Conceptual Framework

Longitudinal case studies conducted by us and others suggested a number of recurring patterns in the differences between successful and unsuccessful strategic moves. As human beings, we have a psychological tendency to see patterns where none may exist statistically, so we discussed the differences between successful and unsuccessful strategic moves extensively in the executive classroom and then refined them more systematically, looking at the histories of two dozen multinational companies. We used hindsight to label each of the big moves made either smart or stupid, depending on how they worked out. In labelling a move smart, or stupid, we tried to correct for forces beyond management's control, such as the collapse of the dotcom bubble, by studying how a comparable company from the same industry and home market performed in the same period. Some big moves were industry firsts, others were in response to shifts in the industry or the business environment and others were responses to company-specific problems.

Five types of big move emerged:

- getting back into shape
- restoring profitability
- going for growth
- relaunching growth
- finding a new game.

The first two of these – getting back into shape and restoring profitability – are about increasing profitability. They typically occur in response to declining margins, caused by company-specific problems, such as a loss of uniqueness, declining efficiency and decreasing access to valuable customers.

Getting back into shape is called for in reaction to the first signs of shrinking margins, well before the problem reaches crisis proportions. It typically involves cutting costs, new processes and streamlining the value chain of activities to provide the platform for profitable growth later on. As we shall see in the case example of HSBC, often it is triggered by the need to digest and integrate an acquisition.

Restoring profitability is about turning around a loss-making situation. It is about more dramatic cutting of costs, divestments and the like to concentrate on the profitable core of the business. While the need to let people go and close down activity is more painful to execute than getting back into shape, the direction required is typically more clear-cut, even if management tries to avoid the pain by forging ahead regardless, as we shall see in the ABB case.

Three of the moves are mainly about improving top-line revenues. Going for growth is about rolling out a business model that works, developing the resources needed to capitalize on positive customer sentiment and ride the growth wave. This is not as obvious as it may seem, as shown by the experience of Apple.

Relaunching growth is about responding to declining growth due, for example, to a slowing market or increasing competition. It typically requires the acquisition of new business or the rejuvenation of the value proposition to serve a well-defined market segment and accelerate growth. As we shall see in the example of Dow Corning, it is about competitive positioning.

Finding a new game is about creating an entirely new business model to replace an existing business that is dying or take advantage of a new technological or market opportunity. It often represents an industry breakthrough – if not globally, then in a particular market, as in the case of Wipro.

Comparing examples of these moves, we arrived at three basic findings that reflect the differences between smart and stupid – that is, successful and unsuccessful big moves. These findings contain what we call the little secrets of great strategic shifts:

- smart strategy
- smart psychology
- smart risk management.

A *smart strategy* embodies the ingredients of successful strategy that are well known in the management literature, but often not implemented. A smart strategy takes advantage of:

- what is distinctive about the company providing a competitive advantage – either capabilities (skills plus process and related culture) and/or positioning (on the demand or supply side) that is sustainable
- significant opportunities for growth that capitalize on the distinctiveness.

Unfortunately, we often do not pursue smart strategies, because our hubris creates a psychological trap that makes us believe that stupid strategies are smart.

*Smart psychology* is about avoiding the psychological traps surrounding big moves. To make a strategic breakthrough, you must have the ambition and courage to take a big step. When we are successful and ambitious, however, we are, once again, prone to hubris – underestimating the challenges in what we are trying to do and overestimating our abilities. Avoiding these related psychological traps is one of the keys to a smart big move. To do so, you have to:

- develop awareness of the psychological traps
- manage your ego and support contrary opinion.

Yet, even when the psychological traps are avoided, a smart strategy still may not be executed because too much risk is taken in the implementation of it.

*Smart risk management* is about ensuring that the move results in a balanced business model, newly developed capabilities are complementary to existing ones and the right implementation process is deployed for the context. To summarize, for smart risk management, we need:

— a balanced business model

— complementary capabilities

— appropriate implementation.

Big moves often disrupt the balance between the resources devoted to the 'what' (value proposition offered to customers), 'who' (customers served) and 'how' (chain of activities used to deliver the value proposition). To get focus and the best return on scarce resources, it is difficult to put equal weight on the what, who *and* how. Yet, success requires that the what, who and how are mutually reinforcing. If not, another move will be needed to restore the balance.

Making a big move happen requires a major commitment of human and financial resources. The supporting capabilities cannot simply be acquired overnight. Even an acquisition takes time to integrate into the existing corporate organization. The less experience the organization has with the new capabilities that are needed, the greater are the chances of failure. The closer the new capabilities are to what the organization already knows how to do, the greater the chances of successful implementation.

A smart implementation process and leadership style capitalizes on and adapts to the forces of change and resistance. It doesn't try to battle needlessly against these forces. For example, big moves with a small window of time for execution demand faster implementation than those that leave more time for deliberate execution. Big moves that face strong resistance require a top-down process to break through the obstacles, whereas when people are able and willing to make the move, a bottom-up process creates commitment.

## How to Read this Book

The first five chapters of *Smart Big Moves* describe the smart strategy, psychology and risk management that are the secrets of the success of the five common strategic shifts. These big moves can happen in any order, depending on the particular circumstances inside and outside the company. A story will provide the context for these five moves – a story about Erik and the company Oaty. Oatly, the real-life Malmö-based company on which the story of Oaty is based, albeit disguised, developed the first oat-based drink on the market. Today, it is the largest player in the oat milk segment in the European market. For our purposes, the story has been dramatized and fictionalized.

The performance curve shown below is a summary of Erik's story and shows the order in which the five moves appear in this book.

**Illustration of the five moves in the performance curve for Oaty.**

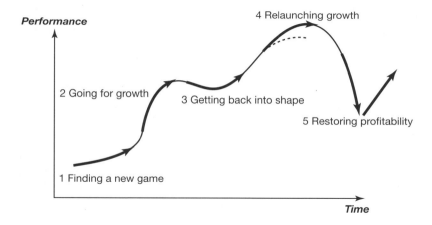

We have illustrated each of the moves with a real-world case study of a company that successfully made a similar move. We comment on how their moves reflect the secrets of smart strategy, psychology and risk management at the end of each chapter of the book. These real-world stories inevitably include several big moves, both smart and stupid, in addition to the one Erik was involved with. Don't be surprised if they are similar to what you have experienced – perhaps all too similar. Look for parallels with what you have seen and draw conclusions about what must be done differently next time.

Finding
a **New Game**
"I can wear
any business suit"

# 1

# Finding a New Game

*Finding a new game* is about creating a new business, or completely rein-venting an old one. It's about departing radically from the past to develop new products, customer segments and a new way of operating – an entirely new business model. You may decide, as we shall see in the case of Wipro, that there is not enough value-creating potential in the existing business and you want to move into a new business. Alternatively, new technology or market developments may open up the opportunity to create a product breakthrough and completely reinvent a business, like Apple's introduction of online music and the iPod. Finding a new game launches a new business performance curve (see below).

**Finding a new game.**

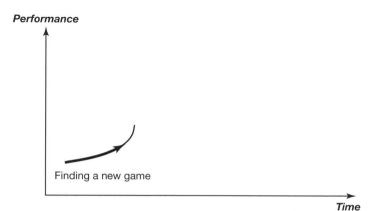

The big psychological trap in finding a new game is to believe you can run any business and therefore take the largest opportunity that presents itself (see Beware Opportunistic Hubris next – excessive self-confidence that makes you believe you can exploit any opportunity). In fact, success depends on recognizing what you can and cannot do. It's not about blind opportunism, but practical entrepreneurship (see Wipro – Opportunism and Experience later in this chapter). You need to reduce the implementation risk by capitalizing on existing expertise, organizational capability or a venture that already exists (see Experience-based Entrepreneurship near the end of this chapter). With experience and resource accessibility in mind, finding a new game calls for a flexible leadership style with the ability to act fast and take advantage of shifting windows of opportunity.

We shall start with Erik's story and see how he found himself looking for a new game and the challenge he faced. In each of the following chapters, we shall continue Erik's story to provide the context for a different type of big move.

## Beware Opportunistic Hubris

Erik caught himself staring out of the window. He looked down at the 50-page document on his desk and its note:

Dear Erik,

As part of our preparation for the Board meeting, please fill in the section on page 38 with your five-year strategic plan, as usual.

Thanks, Tom

The document had been on his desk for 10 days. He looked out of the window again. He realized what he hadn't wanted to admit to himself: this was not going to work.

Erik typed a few lines on his PC, printed and signed the sheet. Paper in hand, he walked slowly but determinedly down the corridor to the CEO's office.

'Stan, my resignation. You can keep the stock options.'

Suddenly he felt free. Considering the sum of money his company had been bought for, the stock option part of the deal was worth less than his freedom. He realized he made a terrible employee.

Stan stared at Erik – disbelief and anger in his eyes, anger he was trying to control.

'Erik, when Software Inc. bought your company, you signed a contract to stay for five years. Not only did we give you a pile of cash but we also gave you stock options, a great office and a great job. What's wrong?'

'Stan, I'm sorry, but I need to run my own thing. Here, any opportunity I want to go for is labelled "too risky", "the market isn't ready for it" and so on.'

'Erik. When we bought your company, we bought *you*. You *can't* leave.'

Erik turned around and walked towards the lifts. He was smiling.

'Erik, Erik. Remember your no competition agreement! Erik?'

Erik smiled even more broadly. He had no intention of staying in the software industry. He was done with software. He was off to conquer the world with a revolutionary product: oat milk.[1]

Erik's first call as he walked out of Software Inc. was to Bjorn – a long-time friend.

'Bjorn, I quit.'

'Well, I could see that coming. You make a terrible employee.'

'I know, I know.'

'So what's next? I've got a couple of neat IT start-ups in the region that could use your expertise.'

'No way. I'm done with that industry. I'm going into oat milk.'

'Oat what? *Milk*? Are you serious?'

'Dead serious. Per called me a couple of weeks ago. He needs some help with his business if he's going to take the product from the lab to the shelves.'

'You're going to join – what's it called, Oaty? It's been around for a couple of years, no?'

'Yep, but they could be doing much better.'

'Aha. Remind me: what's your knowledge of the oat milk business and the consumer goods industry?'

'Irrelevant. They need good old-fashioned business sense, that's all. Think about all those guys we praise today for having been successful outside their own field of expertise: Howard Schultz was a Xerox salesman before he turned Starbucks into the success it is today; Jeff Bezos was an investment banker before launching Amazon. I actually think that my coming in fresh is an asset.'

'OK, OK, I'm not going to push it, but not everyone is Howard Schultz or Jeff Bezos – don't forget those who failed. All the data suggest no more than 1 out of 10 or 20 makes it. What makes the difference is what you bring to the table. Both those guys had skills and/or experience that were key success factors in their new ventures. Drop by on your way home and I'll give you something from my MBA time. It's short and I think you'll find it interesting. It's about how companies create new businesses and reinvent themselves and I think you'll find that what helps companies reinvent is also what helps individuals reinvent.'

The last thing Erik wanted was more reading, but, out of curiosity and respect for his friend, he turned off the road to swing by Bjorn's place.

## Wipro: Opportunism and Experience

It was an evening of celebration in the Svensson household. Viveka, Erik's wife and CEO of her own company, was delighted to hear the news. She too believed that he wasn't cut out for a corporate job, although she had reservations about him joining Per in the oat milk business.

'Viveka, Bjorn thinks like you do. He even gave me this to read.'

He handed Viveka the case that Bjorn had given him earlier on.

## Wipro Ltd

In 1945, M. H. Hasham Premji founded the Western India Vegetable Products (Wipro) company to make vegetable oils and soaps. From the start, Premji stated that his focus was on the customer and on what the customer wanted.[2] In each business, Hasham Premji was careful to put the customer first. He refused an offer from Pakistan's prime minister to become the country's finance minister; instead, he took part of the company public and continued to diversify.

In 1966, Hasham Premji died of a heart attack, barely 6 months before his son, Azim, graduated from Stanford University. At the time of his death, the family business had annual revenues of $3 million, 350 employees and a niche market manufacturing oils, bath soaps and hydraulic fluids. The company's main business was transforming peanuts into cakes and oils.

On his return home, Azim Premji found out that his father had left him the family business. He abandoned his dream of joining the World Bank as a policy-making advocate of the developing world and turned instead to the task of running the family business.[3]

### *Relaunching growth: Azim Premji's 1970s smart big move – repositioning the offering and bringing in new management*

What Premji found was a business that was highly regarded for its ethics but not particularly well run. His father's passion was politics and policymaking, not business. Wipro was publicly traded and investors called on Azim to sell the company to the highest bidder. Convinced that he could make Wipro a success, he set out to modernize the business,[4] putting into practice some of the principles he had come across in the USA. For example, he suggested that the vegetable oil division begin putting the oil into small, company-branded containers to be sold through retailers (bypassing the costly middlemen). This departed significantly from the traditional business model in which customers brought their own containers from home and filled them from open containers in local grocers.

To grow the company, Premji turned to professional managers whom he recruited from top campuses in India. This was a first for a family-run business – typically, relatives constituted the

►

recruitment pool. Premji had no business training, his education being in engineering. In his first year at Wipro, he asked a professor at Bombay's top management school to recommend business books and read them all. He used what he had read to build a company based on leading-edge business policies and practices.

Premji hired his top cadre personally, insisting on meritocracy for both hiring and career progression, using transparent evaluation criteria for determining performance. He built on his father's reputation of integrity and treating employees well and fairly. These practices were revolutionary in early 1970s India and Premji was often asked why he didn't simply follow the accepted standards of paybacks and loopholes. He refused, setting a zero tolerance policy regarding bribes and kickbacks. He also brought measures and processes to a company whose leaders had previously done everything based on tradition and instinct. As Hamm writes, 'He transformed what had been an art into a technology-based business process, which ultimately became one of the company's core competencies.'[5]

### Finding a new game: Premji's 1979–1984 smart big move into hardware distribution, taking advantage of Wipro's distribution and services capabilities

Ten years after he took over, Wipro had become a mini-conglomerate with revenues of $30 million. Premji was ready for more.

In 1977, the Indian government passed a series of rules that forced foreign companies to operate through Indian-owned affiliates. Two years later, IBM left India, due to pressure from the country's socialist government to share its intellectual property. Premji saw the opportunity left by the vacuum and launched Wipro Infotech, a hardware assembly and distribution company that licensed technology from the US-based Sentinel Computer Corporation. Premji hired Sridhar Mitta, who ran the government's satellite-tracking operations, to oversee the new business.

With the technology licensed from Sentinel, Wipro assembled India's first minicomputers. Premji insisted on after-sales service as a key success factor for the business, in much the same way that service had been a hallmark of the vegetable oil business. Premji's competitors tended to hire engineers and teach them sales; he hired business savvy managers who understood service and taught them about the hardware. Wipro quickly became the country's leading computer company. Wipro's reputation for quality and customer service made its computers the obvious choice for many Indian companies.

### Failure to find a new game: Premji's abortive 1984–1985 stupid big move into software development without software expertise

Premji believed that future growth would come not only from hardware but also from software products. However, in the early 1980s, software could not be acquired off the shelf – it had to be developed to clients' specifications. Beginning in 1984, Wipro started developing branded software for its hardware products, but it didn't yet have a software development capability and the venture failed. Nevertheless, Premji persisted, buying an IBM mainframe and developing software for IBM's clients in India.

The company continued to diversify into other areas. Its cooking oil and hydraulic businesses grew and it expanded into babycare products, medical electronics, lighting and finance. In all cases, the company used its strengths in order to diversify: its reputation for integrity, its technology-based business processes and its excellent customer service.

### Finding a new game: Premji's 1995–2000 smart big move into software services, taking advantage of its service capability, the newly developed software capability and an international network of Indian contacts

In the mid-1990s, hardware growth suddenly dropped to 25 per cent. Non-branded PCs – often as much as 30 per cent cheaper than those sold by Wipro – started stealing the market and eating into the company's margins. In addition, the government's new trade liberalization meant that Wipro was competing with the likes of Compaq, Hewlett-Packard and IBM – global giants with virtually infinite R&D budgets and huge sales volumes.

Premji was one of the few Indian business leaders who welcomed foreign competition, believing that it would help raise standards and thus allow Indian companies to compete on a global scale. However, the challenge was to encourage the foreign powerhouses to use the

▶

services of a small, as yet unknown Indian outfit. To gain credibility, in 1995, Wipro obtained its ISO 9000 certification – the International Organization for Standardization (ISO)'s quality standards.

To woo clients, the company sent 'Wipro nomads' to the USA. They would follow leads from fellow Indians spread across the country. They would stay in cheap hotels, go through the phone directory and make cold calls that, more often than not, went unreturned.

The breakthrough came when General Electric, with whom Wipro had a medical equipment joint venture, decided to move some of its software development to India. Wipro won the deal to maintain GE's applications and, later, to develop custom software. By going into the software business and offering business process outsourcing, Wipro rode the wave. 'So twice in a little more than a decade,' Hamm writes, 'Wipro was able to spot fundamental shifts in the business environment and then scramble to create whole new businesses. "It's a core competency for us', says Premji. 'We're able to evaluate opportunities at the right time and put together an act to make a commercial success of it."'[6]

In 1999, Wipro became the world's first company to obtain the Software Engineering Institute's level 5 certification.[7] The decision to go for the toughest certification available was driven by the belief that adopting international quality standards would give Wipro the credibility required to attract multinationals. On top of the certifications, the company applied Toyota's lean manufacturing techniques to software programming and business process outsourcing operations.

By 2000, about 200 of the Fortune 500 were using Indian software services and the industry was growing at an annual rate of 25 to 30 per cent, while Wipro's technology division was growing by 50 per cent annually. In 2000, the company employed 12,500 people, had revenues of $530 million and profits of $69 million. Wipro consisted of 4 divisions:

- Wipro Technologies, which focused on software services for companies based outside India;
- Wipro Infotech, for companies inside India;
- Healthcare Technology Service, a joint venture with GE in medical diagnostic systems;

● Consumer Care and Lighting, including the traditional business of vegetable oils and soaps, as well as toiletries, babycare products and lighting – markets in which Wipro was a medium-sized player; Wipro was also a dominant player in the country's hydraulic cylinder business, but it was a very small contributor to the bottom line.

Approximately 80 per cent of the company's income came from its IT businesses, with 14 per cent from consumer care and lighting. A majority of the company's revenues came from outside India – in fact, three-quarters came from companies based in California.

### Getting back into shape: Premji's 2000–2003 smart big move to realign the management and capabilities of Wipro

Despite its phenomenal success, Wipro was growing more slowly than competitors such as Infosys, and profits in 2000 fell below expectations. The dotcom boom had inspired several of the company's top executives to leave for start-ups. Sridhar Mitta, Premji's top executive, left and took a number of key employees with him, creating a ripple of departures and a general sense of disarray.

Premji took action. To spur growth, he hired a GE executive, Vivek Paul, to make the company more competitive in terms of marketing itself to customers. Paul set clear goals and objectives for the group, delegating authority lower down the hierarchy and defining internal customer service measures.

To support the hyper growth, he reorganized the company, going from independent business units to shared corporate functions and profit and loss responsibility. The company aggressively expanded its capabilities, becoming a major player in business process outsourcing while strengthening its profile on consulting, systems integration and computer data centre management.

### Going for growth: Premji and Paul's mid-2000s smart big move – rolling out software services internationally

Paul felt that Wipro wasn't thinking big enough, that it was still bound by a start-up culture. He set the company an audacious goal, dubbed the '4 in 4' plan: to become a $4 billion company by 2004. To launch the company on that journey, in October 2000, he listed Wipro on the NYSE. Paul planned for half of the company's growth to come from acquisitions; the other half would be organic.

By the end of 2005, Wipro had passed the $1 billion mark in annual revenue and employed 35,000 people. With offices in more than 30 countries, the company had reached its objective of reducing its dependency on the US market, with 67 per cent of its revenues coming from the USA, 27 per cent from Europe and the remaining 6 per cent from Japan and the rest of the world. It was then recognized as one of the world's largest IT product engineering and support service providers.

While falling short of Paul's $4 billion mark, the company had grown into a powerhouse that could seize opportunities and capitalize on them. Growth had been spectacular nonetheless, taking into consideration the 2001–2002 global economic slowdown, which hit the tech industry hard.

Paul left to pursue other challenges in spring 2005. Rather than seek a replacement, Premji himself took charge of the company's tech business. By the end of the financial year 2006, revenue jumped to $2.41 billion and employees were up to 53,000 in 45 countries. By 2007, revenues reached $3.5 billion, up 45 per cent, with profit after tax of $730 million, up 43 per cent.

With the moves into computer hardware and then software services, Azim Premji had reinvented the family business and put it on to a completely new trajectory. He had transformed an old economy company in a local, low-growth industry into a new economy, high growth company spanning the globe. He had turned what was originally seen as a low-cost provider of routine software programming services into a trusted partner to the world's largest companies. 'Tech behemoth Hewlett-Packard in 2005 chose Wipro as one of its global services partners – on the same level as Western giants Accenture and Capgemini.'[8]

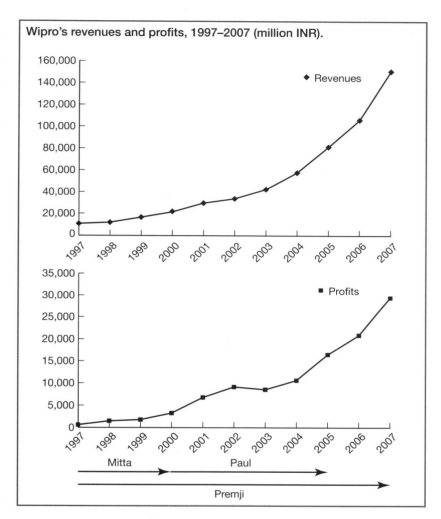

Wipro's revenues and profits, 1997–2007 (million INR).

Erik turned to the last page, which showed Wipro's revenue and profits. On the back of the page, Bjorn had summarized the six distinct phases of the company's trajectory.

## Wipro's phases of development

**1970s** *Relaunching growth – smart big move of repositioning the offering.*

**1979–1984** *Finding a new game – smart big move into hardware distribution.*

**1984–1985** *Failure to find a new game* – stupid big move into software development without software expertise.

**1995–2000** *Finding a new game* – smart big move into software services.

**2001–2003** *Getting back into shape* – smart big move realigning management and capabilities.

**2004–2007** *Going for growth* – smart big move rolling out software services internationally.

## Experience-based Entrepreneurship

Erik smiled at Bjorn's need to share his knowledge. He had enjoyed reading about a company that had managed to reinvent itself so dramatically – after all, going from software to oats wasn't as way out as going from cooking oil to business process outsourcing (BPO). Wipro was also a big, diversified company. He wasn't about to build an outsourcing empire – he was going to focus on one new business. Nothing fancy, just common sense. It was about reinventing one's business activity.

He was slightly annoyed at the note Bjorn had left him: 'Beware of opportunistic hubris, my friend.' What did Bjorn think? This was not opportunistic – this was working with a friend on something that he knew could be successful, if managed properly.

Picking up his mobile, Erik called Bjorn.

'Bjorn, what was the thinking behind the case you sent me?'

'Erik, when I was doing my MBA, I was playing with the idea of a start-up. Then we had this session on entrepreneurship and the thing that stuck in my mind was the way most successful entrepreneurs play to a strength they have. They don't go for the biggest opportunity out there. They work from their strength, inside out to the market, creating their own opportunity and environment. I'm sure I'll be able to dig up my notes. I'll send you an e-mail – a short one, I promise – with a couple of pointers. I can still remember the professor's name – it was Stuart Read.'

'Thanks. I do think I know a thing or two about that, Bjorn, but send me your notes anyway – I'm curious!'

When he read Bjorn's e-mail later, he could only agree with its advice, knowing that he had done many of these things instinctively:

- Start with your means. Take action based on what you (the firm) have available (what you have, what you know, whom you know) instead of trying to set goals to reach some optimal position.

- Set an affordable loss limit. Pursue interesting opportunities without investing more resources than you can afford to lose. Set a limit on downside potential.

- Form partnerships. Strategy is created jointly with stakeholders that create new opportunities where everyone who commits benefits.

- Leverage the context. Surprises are good. New developments encourage imaginative rethinking of possibilities and continual transformation of targets.

- Don't try to predict the future — it's about as reliable as predicting the weather. Instead, try to shape it. Create an environment where you will have an advantage.

Erik got back on the phone to Bjorn.

'Bjorn, I'm doing all five of those things already with Per. Anything else I should have noticed in the Wipro case study?'

'Well, one of the things I like about the Wipro story is the way they reinvented themselves in the 1990s based on their hardware distribution business, services capability and newly developed software know-how. By building on what they already had, they turned a big bet into a much surer move. That way they increased their chances of success and went on to become one of the world's largest business process outsourcing and software services companies.'

'True, but Wipro had an existing business base. We'll be starting almost from scratch, with a single product.'

'That should actually give you an advantage. Compared with those of us in big companies, you won't have to reinvent an existing organization. At Wipro, Premji jumped through the windows of opportunity created, first, by IBM's departure and, second, by India's reintegration into the world economy, but then Wipro had to put in place a completely new business model in line with those it was targeting as customers, what it was offering the market – the value proposition – and how it was delivering it – the value chain of activities involved.'

'Bjorn, if Per agrees to work with me, we'll have no choice but to look at who, what and how we do oat milk. You MBA guys just dress the obvious up in fancy language.'

Bjorn laughed.

'I can understand that you might not like the buzzwords, so let me send you a chart instead, OK? I think you will like this one.'

Erik had always thought that big company MBA guys invariably made simple points complex, but he liked what he saw coming up on his screen.

**Finding a new game: create a new business model.**

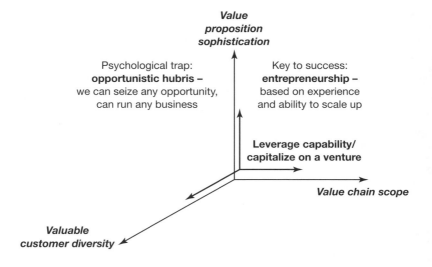

Bjorn continued.

'What you see is that, typically, successful new business models are built on either existing capability or an existing venture. To avoid making a big bet with high chances of failure, successful companies look in-house before jumping. Think about how Nokia did it. They had a small mobile business that they decided to capitalize on. They sold off all of their legacy businesses – tyres, boots, a mix of electronics – and focused their resources on the new venture. IBM did the same thing when it went into services and it's what Wipro did when it added a software capability to its hardware distribution business and then moved into software services.'

'It's what you call capitalizing on a venture?'

'Yes.'

'What about leveraging a capability?'

'That's what Wipro did when it built its first hardware business on after-sales service, taking advantage of the service skills, process and culture it had developed in the oils business. Premji was also smart enough to bring in people who complemented his management style. It's starting with what you have, whether you're a large corporation or an entrepreneur. The successful ones avoid falling into opportunistic hubris – they don't confuse dreams with reality. They don't take the first opportunity that comes along and think they can run anything, or get trapped by wishful thinking, jumping into something because everyone else is doing it or because it's a sexy new industry.'

Bjorn paused.

'There is something else.'

'What?' Erik asked.

'You'll have to think about your role. If you're going to make this work, you'll need to be quite directive and force a number of decisions top-down – especially to ensure that Oaty moves beyond pioneering and scales up the business to get volume. Be careful, too, not to crush the existing creativity. The R&D lab at Oaty is known for coming out with stuff that is truly original and it is one of their strongest assets. I suspect that Oaty may have worked in a very collaborative manner so far, but might need a bit more of a "commander" at this point. You'll have to tread a careful balance between continuing to support that creativity and getting things done so that they really get their product on the market and capitalize on their first mover advantage.'

It was Eric's turn to laugh.

'Thanks, Bjorn. I think being tough on execution is one thing I should be OK with.'

## Secrets of Finding a New Game

The psychological trap is that we think we can seize any opportunity, run any business.

When we're successful, it's only natural to assume that, while the context may have been a factor, our intelligence and leadership have been central to the outcome. When we're lucky enough to have been repeatedly successful and rise to the top, we are easily convinced that our intelligence and leadership are well above average – that we would have got there no matter what the context, and that with enough commitment and energy, we can make a success of almost any business.

As we saw when Erik sold out his software business, he was riding high and had little inclination to play the role of a manager, still less submit to the bureaucracy of a large company. In his mind, there was no doubt that he could make a success of an oat milk business, no matter how far-fetched that may have seemed to Bjorn.

Similarly, at Wipro, after Premji's huge success in moving from vegetable oils and soap into computer hardware distribution, he felt sure that there was no reason for not moving the company into software development. Once he started making the move, however, it became clear that software development was a very different animal from hardware distribution. Wipro had to get on to a new learning curve.

### Smart Psychology

*When trying to find a new game, the smart psychology is to get feedback from someone with start-up or venture capital experience, especially on the appropriate mix of managerial expertise and industry-specific capabilities.*

Erik was lucky to have Bjorn to alert him to the psychological trap. He was also intuitively smart enough to contain his ego and enter into a wide-open dialogue with Bjorn.

At Wipro, Azim Premji had the advantage of the norms his father had established – not only in terms of the company's ethics but also a concern for larger policy issues beyond those affecting its own immediate interests. Seeing a bigger picture helps to put one's own accomplishments into perspective. Note, however, that it wasn't enough to save Premji from misjudging the software challenge.

## Smart Strategy

*Making the stretch to start a new game only makes sense when the new value proposition is truly distinctive and the upside growth potential is really large.*

For Erik, Oaty had the advantage of being a first mover in oat milk and, for a start-up, the demand for lactose-free milk seemed very large.

When IBM left India, the supply vacuum it left behind was huge. For those locals with their eyes open and a distribution capability in place, it created a golden opportunity to simply replace IBM in the market with imported machines. As the competition intensified, Premji recognized the need to find a new game and the size of the opportunity in software. However, Wipro couldn't deliver a viable value proposition, let alone a distinctive one. Going immediately to market with homemade software was precocious, but not smart. Equally, once Wipro became the first company in the world to acquire the Software Engineering Institute's level 5 certification, it had something truly distinctive and the opportunity worldwide for outsourced information services was enormous.

## Smart Risk Management

*In finding a new game, you have to balance the focus on product and value proposition development with customer acquisition and delivery capability.*

Erik's arrival at Oaty would help to rebalance the business model by adding marketing and operations expertise to Per's R&D.

At Wipro, Azim Premji, as an engineer, also had a professional bias towards product development. However, he recognized early on the need to rebalance the business model with best management practice and, later, made two organizational moves – first, into business divisions and, later, shared functions – to integrate the organization and improve efficiency.

*In terms of capabilities, executing a new game requires entrepreneurship based on experience.*

At Oaty, Per would provide the technical know-how that Erik lacked. From Erik's perspective, Per's start-up was an existing new venture with the technical experience needed to develop a new game.

In a classic complementary move, Wipro added hardware services to its already well-developed customer service capability and distribution network. The later attempt to add software development was not a simple complement to customer service, however. Wipro had to acquire that capability the hard way, incrementally building it up through hard-won experience with IBM clients. Then, to leverage its distribution into the global market, it added new complementary capabilities in business process outsourcing, consulting, systems integration and computer data centre management.

*In terms of leadership and implementation, the challenge in finding a new game is to inspire the creativity and follow up with a focus on execution.*

Erik would have to adapt his commander style to maintain the space for ongoing product development bottom-up, while providing the top-down direction to get the product to market.

Premji was sufficiently self-aware to complement his entrepreneurial drive with additional management skills to assist with the implementation of some of the big moves, especially in terms of getting the company into shape to prepare it for subsequent growth. Early on, he brought in professional managers to put in basic management practice. Then, he hired Sridhar Mitta to bring the technical expertise and lead the move into hardware distribution. Later on, prior to the international roll-out, he hired Vivek Paul from GE to integrate the organization with shared corporate functions and performance-based management.

Finding a new game is the big move that involves the greatest discontinuity with the past and, hence, the greatest risk of failure. To make that risk worth taking, it's essential that the potential reward is large enough, in the form of a truly distinctive value proposition that addresses a sizeable market. To keep the risk manageable, it is important not to underestimate the challenge and to ensure that you take advantage of an existing venture or existing capability or first build the necessary capability incrementally. Then, ensure focus and cost-effective delivery.

# Going
# for **Growth**

## "I know what customers want"

# 2

# Going for Growth

*Going for growth* is about focusing resources on a profitable business model and rolling it out to gain market share in existing markets and move into adjacent segments, plus new geographies. This usually carries the lowest risk of all the big moves and has led to many of the most successful periods of value creation – Apple's roll-out of the Mac, iTunes and the iPod, for example. In Apple's case, these roll-outs followed the finding of a new game. However, depending on the circumstances, roll-outs could follow any of the other big moves. In the late 1990s, Steve Jobs at Apple rolled out new products after restoring profitability. At Wipro, the international roll-out of software services followed a move to get back into shape. In Erik's story, roll-out to the European market would follow his arrival at Oaty.

**Going for growth.**

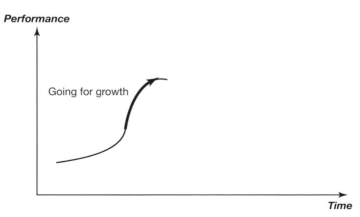

The psychological trap in going for growth is believing that you and your people are the experts and know what customers want in the new market; you don't have to waste time finding out (see Beware Inside-out Projection next – projecting beliefs from inside the company out on to customers). In fact, one of the secrets to high levels of growth is a value proposition exactly tailored to customers' wants, creating much more value for them than the competitors' offerings (see Apple: Not Projection but Customer Value Creation later in this chapter). Successful roll-out depends on deep, sensitive observation and understanding of what customers want. This may mean that the value proposition has to be fine-tuned to fit the wants of other high-growth segments (see Value-creating Roll-out near the end of the chapter). On the leadership side, roll-out calls for the training and development of sufficient talent to support it and enough freedom on the front line to pursue the unfolding market opportunities.

# Beware Inside-out Projection

The phone rang. Per hesitated to pick it up. Probably another call about an unpaid bill. He looked around the lab, trying to locate the phone.

'Per, it's Erik.'

Per answered, relieved.

'Hi. Thought it was more bad news.'

'I quit the company. Are you still doing the oat thing?'

'I sure am, although I'm not sure how much longer I can manage. I like the R&D part, but I find deciding what the market may or may not want a bit of a mystery. My offer to you still stands. I need your help.'

'I'm on my way.'

As he made his way to the Underground, Erik thought about Per. Per was a brilliant chemist who had come up with a formula for turning oats into oat milk. The product was a fantastic substitute for milk's for people who are lactose-intolerant: its taste was smoother than soya milk's and it provided a great new outlet for the oats that grow in large quantities in central and southern Sweden. He knew he could bring to the table the business experience needed and that, together, they could turn this product into a real winner. He would make sure that the company focused on getting its products out there and Per could continue doing what he liked best – being the creative drive behind the company's innovations.

That same afternoon, the two friends agreed to work together.

☆ ☆ ☆

In the first few weeks after Erik joined the company, he worked hard on the visibility of the Oaty brand. He and Per met with retailers and healthfood shops, studied consumers' profiles and looked at market trends. Erik used his contacts and relative fame as an entrepreneur – he had been the star of the Swedish business press after his successful venture into software – to get the company's name into the press. He negotiated hard with a new retailer that promised to take a proactive stance in marketing the oat milk in its shops. Its midsummer slogan 'The day after' had been a huge hit.

Erik also believed that people wanted variety, something that suited their particular tastes. He persuaded Per to get the company's chemists working on a new product: loganberry-flavoured oat milk. Erik had a difficult time convincing Per.

'Remember Absolut, Per. All vodkas are basically the same. What helped them sell Absolut? A great package and creative flavours. We need to be the non-alcoholic Absolut.'

'I hear you, but Absolut had a single flavour for a long time. Do we need to do this right away?'

Despite Per's doubts, he had to acknowledge that Erik had been right about his first decision on joining the business – changing retailers, moving from single store outlets to food chains. The strategy had almost tripled the company's revenue and it could barely keep up with the orders coming in from ICA – one of the largest Scandinavian chains. Per had to trust Erik's business instincts.

☆ ☆ ☆

Within two years of Erik's arrival, Oaty had made it to the top of the chart for alternative milk drinks. Sales were growing. Per was ecstatic.

Erik, however, was unhappy: his brainchild – loganberry Oaty – had failed to catch on. He couldn't understand it. The company was using Sweden's national berry – beloved by the country's consumers – for its primary brand extension, yet shoppers were walking past the loganberry Oaty. He put the statistics sheets down. He was already late for his lunch meeting with Per and Bjorn.

Sitting down at the table, Erik couldn't take his mind off the loganberry Oaty.

'Bjorn, I just don't get it.'

Bjorn looked at his friend.

'Sounds like the New Coke story to me. Inside-out projection.'

'What do you mean?'

'Well, the classic example of this kind of inside-out projection is Coca-Cola's bomb with New Coke in 1985. Pepsi was catching up. Coke's CEO, Roberto Goizueta, decided that radical action was required. He changed the recipe for the first time in a century. They did exhaustive blind taste tests and people said that they liked New Coke more than traditional Coke and Pepsi, but, to keep it all a marketing surprise, there were no test runs. After the launch, the market rose up in rebellion against the new taste: "Coke for wimps", "Changing Coke is like God making grass purple", "You've taken away my childhood", "How could you destroy something that took 99 years to build?". You get the idea. Even Coca-Cola's resident historian, Phil Rooney, said, "We totally underestimated the emotional bond the public had with our brand. This brand was part of American popular culture and suddenly we took it away."'

Erik interrupted.

'I remember New Coke. It was terrible. How did it end?'

'Well, Coke was lucky that its customers cared enough to protest. After about 80 days and 400,000 letters and phone calls, management announced the return of the old formula as Coke Classic. Sales rose and the share price increased by a third during the following year. The CEO got to keep his job – just.'

'I see, but I'm not sure about this inside-out projection thing. Sounds like more of your MBA jargon to me.'

'It's a classical trap: projecting your beliefs about what the market wants on to your roll-out. Instead, you need to start with what the market likes about your value proposition, where you are already making money, then work from the outside in, translating what customers want into your roll-out. With loganberry Oaty, you launched a flavour that no one asked for. Your consumers enjoy your plain flavour – why do more at this point?'

Per, who had remained silent, nodded.

'You're saying we got carried away?'

'The biggest problem with what you've started doing is that, if you don't focus and put all of your resources into the roll-out of the product that *does* work, you will lose out. The company's energy will be spread out in different directions and people won't know what to focus on. Also Erik, at this stage you probably want to make sure that you have full buy-in from your people, rather than imposing a new product top-down. Remember, the best measure of what the success is is where you're making money. I haven't seen your figures, but I'll bet that plain Oaty is paying for loganberry Oaty at the moment.'

Erik hated to admit it, but he could see Bjorn's point. The market wasn't ready for a multitude of oat milks and they were definitely losing money with the loganberry flavour.

Back at the plant, Erik and Per considered their options. It would be expensive to discontinue the loganberry option now.

Per spoke his mind.

'Erik, I think Bjorn is right. We need to cut our losses. Our cash flow is suffering. We were thinking too big too soon.'

'I don't know. I know people want variety. When I was in software, people were always asking for modifications, for something slightly different, every customer had unique needs, and I'm sure it's the same here. *I* want diversity – *everyone* wants diversity.'

'Erik, this isn't software. This is a drink. Don't forget the farmers' cooperative. Whether we like it or not, they own half of this company and they're not happy with what's happening to our cash flow. This is my product, my company and I want to make sure *everyone* is happy.'

'Traditionalists, the whole lot. They have no idea.'

Suddenly, there was a rap on the door.

'Express package for Mr Erik Svensson.'

A fat yellow envelope was handed over to Per. The two men looked at each other. More trouble?

## Apple: Not Projection but Customer Value Creation

Opening the envelope, Per swore.

'What on earth? This is a bit much. Does he really think we have time for this? On Apple, of all things. If at least it had been on soya milk ... especially after all his talk at lunch about focusing and not being arrogant ...'

Erik sighed, taking the documents from Per.

'OK, I have nothing planned for tonight anyway. Give it to me.'

---

### Apple Inc.

#### *Dispute over optimistic projections*

John Sculley joined Apple in 1983, hired away from Pepsi by Steve Jobs with the now-famous words, 'Are you going to sell sugar water for the rest of your life when you could be doing something really important?'[1] Sculley was hard to convince, but he finally took the job – largely because he admired Jobs as a business leader. The Board approved Sculley as President as it believed that he could control Jobs and mentor him.

At first, Sculley bought into Jobs' optimistic projections for the newly released Macintosh, but soon fights between the two men threatened to tear the company apart. Jobs, as head of both the Macintosh and Lisa projects, blamed Sculley for the continuously falling sales, arguing that he did not understand how to run the company. In reality,

---

people were not buying the Mac because there were not enough available software applications. By the end of 1984, 200,000 machines were liquidated through a bartering company.

By March 1985, sales for the Macs were running at 10 per cent of the projected figure. Sculley found it impossible to run a company in which he was pitted against the founder and Chairman of the Board. A month later, the Board asked Sculley to take charge. On 28 May, after a number of failed coups against Sculley, Jobs was asked to leave the company.

*Going for growth: Sculley's 1985–1990 smart big move – completing the Macintosh value proposition and focusing resources on the roll-out*

As a consumer products man, Sculley had been impressed by the Macintosh's technical performance. To achieve its growth potential, he knew that Apple would have to encourage the development of Mac-specific software by opening up some of the proprietary code to third-party developers. With Jobs out of the picture, Sculley was free to work on turning the company round. He reorganized Apple, focusing on the Macintosh and killing the Lisa project, which had drained resources for years without leading to anything. Riding the roll-out wave of the Mac, Apple had some of its best years through to the late 1980s.

*Failure to relaunch growth: Sculley's 1990–1993 stupid big move – not accepting the market's verdict that the Macintosh value proposition was too expensive and diversifying into the crowded consumer electronics market*

The turn of the decade, from the 1980s to the 1990s, was a period of intense price competition. Compaq launched the PC wars by suddenly slashing its prices, sending its competitors scrambling to do the same – all of them except Apple. Sculley refused to cut prices.

Instead, Apple began diversifying into the consumer electronics market. In January 1990, Sculley announced the roll-out of three multimedia product lines, involving software that Apple would license to other consumer electronics companies for use in their products, as well as a third line of products focused on personal information devices. The announcement heralded a basic shift in the company's approach. 'In the '80s, Apple sold overpriced hardware and gave away neat software for free', Sculley said. 'In the '90s, Apple's objective is to sell really cheap hardware so it can sell more software.'[2] Sculley was determined to apply the same ease-of-use philosophy that guided the Mac to everything from televisions to telephones.

Unfortunately for Apple, the consumer electronics market was dominated by aggressive competitors with thin margins. The diversification stepped on the toes of makers of video games, electronic organizers and mobile phones. Making the company's operating software available to others also challenged Microsoft. Apple was trying to crash the consumer electronics party and the others already there were not happy.

To make matters worse, consumers were no longer willing to pay a premium for the user-friendly Macintosh. Microsoft's Windows software offered a reasonable facsimile of the Mac's user-friendliness at a much lower price, on cheaper computers. Thus, by the spring of 1993, $1.2 billion worth of Macintoshes were gathering dust in warehouses. Consumers were flocking en masse to the new IBM PCs. *The Economist* lamented:

> *How could a company with smart people, nifty technology and born-again followers in the marketplace make such a mess of things? Apple Computer is in the throes of the biggest crisis in its 17-year history. In July the company reported a third-quarter loss of $188m. Since then, Apple has seen its market capitalization drop by more than half. Financial analysts say the computer maker will be lucky to produce net profits of $295m on sales of $7.9 billion for the year ending this September. Last year Apple had twice the profit margin, earning $530m on revenue of $7.1 billion.[3]*

Apple seemed doomed again, caught in its proprietary cul-de-sac. In October 1993, John Sculley left Apple, with a going away gift of $4 million. The company agreed to buy his $4 million house and his Learjet. Apple USA President Robert Puette also resigned. In November, Shigechika Takeuchi abruptly quit as President of Apple Japan, the company's most successful subsidiary.

*Failure to relaunch growth: Spindler's 1994–1995 stupid big move – believing Apple could compete in the business market, where design has little value, and continuing the drive into consumer electronics*

The Board replaced John Sculley with his second-in-command, Michael Spindler, and openly hoped that the management shake-up would create a new, more agile management team.

Spindler, whose 18-hour work days earned him the nickname 'The Diesel', was a hard-driving salesman who knew how to cut costs. He took immediate action, cutting the salaries of senior management, freezing all other salaries and firing 2500 employees – 17 per cent of the workforce. He also slashed prices by as much as 35 per cent. Apple's margins dropped from over 50 per cent to 23 per cent, which was comparable with those of Compaq.

For the first time in its history, Apple tried to compete on price rather than style. Spindler believed that Apple could compete in the larger PC market (office and business) – a market in which style is irrelevant and price and performance are paramount. It didn't work.

Spindler also made the mistake of continuing Apple's drive into consumer electronics. In November 1993, the company launched the multimedia MacTV, which was aimed at homes, small offices and university students' rooms. However, competitors had already introduced computers with TV functionality, so the MacTV failed to find a foothold.

Spindler's turnaround moves improved profits temporarily, but failed to address the problems inherent in Apple's high-cost business model. As the *Financial Times* observed:

> *By distancing itself from the herd with its proprietary Macintosh system, Apple has had to develop practically all its own hardware and write (and rewrite) its own operating system, the internal software that lets a computer do useful things ... Thus while Apple has had to spend between 8 and 10% of its revenue on research and development (a staggering $600m last year), rivals such as Compaq, Dell and Gateway 2000 have got away with spending 2% or less on R&D.[4]*

▶

Spindler decided that only a white knight could save Apple and approached both Sun Microsystems and Philips Electronics. In late 1995, as negotiations with Sun reached a delicate point, Apple announced its worst ever results for the year ending that September. By December, the share price had fallen by almost 20 per cent.

Sun's CEO, Scott McNealy, backed out of the ongoing negotiations and Apple's Board members started looking for a new CEO.

**Restoring profitability: Amelio's 1996–1997 smart big move – restructuring top-down, interrupted by the cultural trap sprung by Apple's development engineers**

The Board turned to one of its own, Gil Amelio, who had argued that the company could be saved from bankruptcy. He was asked to take on the role of CEO in February 1996. Amelio, a physicist and co-author, with William L. Simon, of the best-selling *Profit from Experience: Practical, proven skills for transforming your organization* (Van Nostrand Reinhold, 1995), was President and CEO of National Semiconductor, a company he had rescued from near bankruptcy in a little less than three years.

Amelio reorganized Apple, adopting a functional structure with four divisions to replace the existing product line division. He continued Spindler's restructuring and managed to stem the flow of red ink. He wrote off inventory and fired 15 per cent of the company's workforce, which boosted the cash flow.

Serious problems were emerging with Apple's proprietary operating system (OS), however, and Amelio realized that a new OS was Apple's best chance of recapturing momentum and market share. Unfortunately, the people he brought from National Semiconductor to support him didn't mesh with the freewheeling Apple engineers. The command-and-control style did not go down well with the 'pirates'.

Having given up on Apple's in-house product development team, Amelio started looking outside for a viable alternative. Sun was approached, along with Be Inc., founded by former Apple man Jean-Louis Gassée. Bill Gates contacted Apple. Then engineers from NeXT, Jobs' new software firm, approached the company. Apple developers rated all four operating systems, but chose

NeXT's – not surprising given that Apple's development culture was still the one Jobs had created and the man himself put on a charismatic and persuasive show for his old colleagues.

Amelio was now trapped by the old Apple culture, compelled to incorporate NeXT software and hire Steve Jobs as a special adviser. Jobs immediately placed his NeXT lieutenants in key hardware and software roles. When Apple's annual loss came in at around $1 billion, Jobs lobbied the Board to fire Amelio, insisting that he alone could save the company. In July 1997, Amelio was asked to leave – less than 18 months after agreeing to take the top job. When he had stepped in, the company had barely enough cash to survive for three months. When he left, Apple had over $3 billion in cash.

***Going for growth: Jobs' 1998–2000 smart big move – leveraging Apple's core design capability to roll out new products in the loyal consumer market***

In December 1997, Apple announced that it was acquiring NeXT and invited Jobs to take the title of Interim Chief Executive. He continued Amelio's turnaround strategy, slashing products and product lines aggressively, including the Newton – a much ballyhooed PDA that Apple had spent years developing. He outsourced the OS and, later, most of the company's manufacturing so that it could scale down without laying off employees. By January 1998, the turnaround initiated by Amelio was complete and Apple was back in the black.

In parallel, Jobs launched a set of products, including a snazzy new desktop computer dubbed the iMac. Jobs signalled that he would refocus Apple on what it did best: build beautiful computers at premium prices. The market loved it.

The visionary, charismatic Jobs was hailed for having understood and captured a market that craved individuality. Apple continued expanding its product line, introducing iBooks, PowerBooks and PowerMac G4s. Apple's engineers also designed a port that made wireless networking child's play. The fact that Apple still designed all of its hardware and most of its own software now meant that the company was often seen as setting the standard for what a PC should be like. New York's Museum of Modern Art made it official by enshrining several Macintoshes as examples of exceptional design and engineering.

In a *Fortune* essay, venture capitalist Stewart Alsop announced his return to the fold:

*Like most people, I wrote the Macintosh off a long time ago. After an 11-year relationship, I dumped the Mac in 1996 and persuaded my partners to switch to a Windows-only network. I thought Apple Computer was pretty much toast. But then Steve Jobs refocused the employees and started getting real financial results, and the company delivered a series of truly cool devices. All of which led me, a few weeks ago, to buy my first Apple product in years – the gorgeous Titanium G4 Macintosh. Now I'm rethinking the Macintosh as a factor in computing. There's one simple reason: unlike Windows, the Macintosh seems to work.*[5]

Then the dotcom bubble burst. On 30 September 2000, Apple lost $8.5 billion in market cap. The dot-bomb didn't kill the company, though, which it surely would have done had it struck three years earlier. In adapting to the burst bubble, Apple proved to be the industry's most well-balanced company.

During the PC industry's worst ever slump, Apple continued to churn out innovative products and entirely revamp its product lines. Apple's titanium PowerBook laptop, launched in January 2001, became its best-selling product since the Macintosh. Two months later, Apple introduced the OS X operating system – a system that was not only highly stable and reliable but also allowed for easier sharing of Mac and Windows files. It also launched a slew of multimedia products – iDVD, iMovie, iPhoto and others – as part of an overall strategy to make Mac the heart of the networked world.

***Finding a new game: Jobs' 2001–2003 smart big move – acquiring complementary software and hardware to create a new business model in the fast-growing market for downloaded music***

To make the digital hub strategy really work, Jobs believed that he needed something 'stunningly new', Digital cameras, camcorders and organizers had highly competitive and well-established competitors, but the digital music field was surprisingly open. Digital music players were lacking in quality. Napster, the highest-profile firm, peaked in February 2001, but was hamstrung by legal challenges and soon shut down altogether. Apple's industry scouts turned to SoundJam MP – the most popular Mac software audio player, developed by Casady & Greene with help from Apple engineers. Apple threatened to develop a competing product if Casady & Greene did not sell it the rights. Apple did more than buy the software, though: it raided Casady & Greene for its top people.

On 9 January 2001, Apple introduced iTunes music- and video-management software at the annual MacWorld Expo. Jobs beamed, declaring, 'iTunes is miles ahead of every other jukebox application.'

Then, with impeccable timing, an itinerant engineer, Tony Fadell, knocked on Apple's door bearing the basics of a hand-held music player. Fadell had first taken his device to RealNetworks, but Jobs turned out to be far more receptive. Jobs took the offer and gave Apple's engineers the same deadline as the iTunes team – less than 12 months to develop a new music player.

The hand-held that Apple put together was based on an existing product from a semiconductor company called PortalPlayer. The design, however, was pure Apple. Jobs unveiled the iPod on 23 October 2001, and from then on, for millions of people, Apple would no longer be primarily a computer company.

### Going for growth: Jobs' mid-2000s smart big move – completing the online music value proposition and rolling it out

In April 2003, Apple launched the iTunes Store, running the iTunes application on PCs as well as Macs. Relative to competing products, it compressed songs quickly, allowed easy creation of playlists and connected easily to online streaming radio stations. *Time* (17 November 2003) called it 'the coolest invention of 2003'.

By 2006, unit sales of iPods accounted for the majority of Apple products sold. The product captured over 90 per cent of the market share in the digital music hardware market,[6] despite a 15 to 20 per cent premium over other MP3 players (its market share went from 28 per cent in 2003 to 66 per cent in 2004) and 70 per cent market share for all types of players. Rio was second with just 2.8 per cent of the market. The iTunes Store had sold more than 2 billion songs, accounting for 75 per cent of worldwide online digital music sales.

In 2007, Apple sold 7 million Macs and 51 million iPods – both up more than 30 per cent from 2006 – for a total revenue of $24 billion – up by 24 per cent – and net income of $3.5 billion – up by 75 per cent compared with the previous year. The year 2007 was also the year in which Apple moved into the crowded mobile phone market with the iPhone, which was designed to be a personal communications hub.

## Value-creating Roll-out

Erik leaned back into the sofa. So far, the case had been a great read. What was interesting was how these successful companies were not consistently great over time – they made mistakes and were victims of the shortcomings of human nature. Apple's smartest moves had been when it had capitalized on existing knowledge and competencies and gave the market what it wanted. Its stupid moves were linked to ego and hubris – CEOs believing that they knew best. At the same time, Erik liked the fact that Jobs knew exactly what he wanted, took control and imposed his vision on the company. He created a sense of urgency that drove the company forward. Maybe that is what he should have done with the loganberry Oaty, but he found it difficult to impose decisions on the company with Per always wanting to involve everyone.

On the last page of the case, Erik found notes scribbled by Bjorn, probably from a class discussion:

Avoiding inside-out projection

- Create additional personal bandwidth (concept developed by Jean-François Manzoni[7]) – mental space to see, listen and understand what's really going on, especially the undercurrents and deeper market trends:
  - open up time in your schedule;
  - put new activities on the agenda;
  - expose yourself to different types of people, those willing to question your opinions – two 'yes men' is one too many.

- Work from the outside in:
  - get feedback from the front line – expand your circle of regular contacts;
  - put yourself in the shoes of your customers;
  - get out into the market, test out their reactions.

- Be open to facts that don't fit your preconceptions:
  - don't rationalize away uncomfortable data;
  - integrate it into your thinking and – this is the big challenge – even if it means abandoning your pet project;
  - ensure the market facts are consistent with value creation – for both your customers and your company.

Erik put the case study down. What had he learned? Instinctively, he dialled.

'Hi, Bjorn, about this Apple story ...'

'Erik? It's past midnight! Do you know what normal people do at night? They *sleep*.'

With that, Bjorn hung up.

Erik made more coffee. It was probably not a good idea to call Per either, although he was probably still at the lab. He switched on his PowerBook and typed 'Apple history' into the search engine. There were thousands of articles on the iconic company.

As the hours went by and he kept reading, he realized why Bjorn had given him the story. Every time Apple was close to failing, it had been because someone had thought he knew better than the market what the market wanted.

Was his own past experience making him behave in a similar way?

In the company's early days, Steve Jobs fell repeatedly into the trap of projecting his beliefs on to the market. For him, it was all about launching sexy new products. The Board had had to intervene to give John Sculley the opportunity to make the smart big move and roll out the golden, low business risk opportunity that lay waiting: the Mac. In the end, it wasn't hardware but sexy new software that saved both NeXT and Apple over and over again.

When the computer wars hit, Sculley was carried away by grandiose illusions about what Apple could do in consumer electronics. His big diversification move was a big bet that failed because it didn't make Apple distinct from the competitors in consumer electronics. Neither did it address the big operating risk in Apple's model – its high-cost R&D structure. As a result, the diversification drive could not create real value for customers. Erik was struck by a comment that he ran across on the Web: 'Apple's decision not to license the Macintosh system goes down as perhaps the most expensive business error in history' (Lex column, *Financial Times*, 8 May 1996). What a missed opportunity!

Erik also realized that the CEOs who followed Sculley had not learned from his mistake. Michael Spindler continued with Sculley's folly. An apparent victim of Apple's belief that it was special and 'knew' what customers wanted, Spindler's turnaround plan did not call into question any of Apple's different divisions, not even the one responsible for the Newton MessagePad disaster.[8] More fatal for Spindler, as an outsider and a foreigner – he was German – was his belief that he could put his plan into effect without solid support from the Board. At the first sign of difficulties, it dumped him.

Thinking of his own situation, Erik knew that he was seen as an outsider by those in the farmers' cooperative. They snubbed rather than admired him for being an engineer and, on top of that, an engineer who had 'sold his soul' to Americans when he gave up ownership of the software company he had founded.

It was Gil Amelio's experience that resonated most with Erik, though. Amelio had believed that he could transpose his experience at National Semiconductor on to Apple; he didn't see how different the cultures were. His fate was sealed by an inadequate change process that relied more on forcing people to accept change than on encouraging them to embrace it. He also completely misjudged the level of support he had from those on the Board and how wily Jobs could be.[9]

Was he, Erik, doing the same thing? Was he relying too much on his experience with Software Inc. and underestimating how different the culture at Oaty was?

Apple's list of both successful and unsuccessful new products – from the Apple II to the Lisa, Macintosh, Newton, iMac, iMovie, iPod and iTunes – all pointed in the same direction: away from products alone and towards the design and creation of a unique customer experience. The company turned big bets into surer moves by incrementally developing new capabilities. Thus, it was poised to take advantage of market opportunities when they emerged. In launching and rolling out iTunes and the iPod, Jobs knew that Napster had created a large market for downloadable music and that no product in the market – including Napster, then already under fire – was user-friendly. Apple could create not only real value for customers but also an industry breakthrough by leveraging available technology with its cool brand image, user-friendly software and ability to create excitement in the market. On the other hand, the move into the crowded, highly competitive, mobile phone market was likely to be much more challenging, unless Apple could position itself as a unique mobile communications hub.

Erik went back to the chart in the case that showed the company's trajectory over the course of the CEO's tenures and read Bjorn's notes.

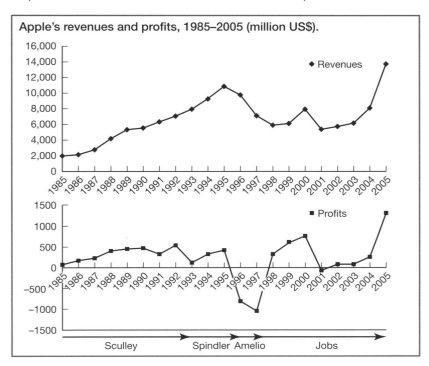

Apple's revenues and profits, 1985–2005 (million US$).

## Apple's phases of development

- **1985–1990** *Going for growth* – smart big move of rolling out the Mac.

- **1991–1993** *Failure to relaunch profitable growth* – stupid big move diversifying into consumer electronics.

- **1994–1995** *Failure to relaunch growth* – stupid big move trying to compete in the business market.

- **1996–1998** *Restoring profitability* – smart big move of restructuring started by Amelio and completed by Jobs.

- **1998–2000** *Going for growth* – smart big move of rolling out new products in loyal customer segments.

- **2001–2003** *Finding a new game* – smart big move of creating a new business model in the fast-growing market for online music.

- **2004–2006** *Going for growth* – smart big move of rolling out iTunes and the iPod.

Three of the big moves – in 1985, 1998 and 2004 – were smart, value-creating roll-outs, followed by strongly rising sales and profits. Two – in 1991 and 1994 – were unsuccessful attempts to project internal beliefs about what the market wanted on to the marketplace, followed by declining profits.

As the dawn light streamed into his living room, Erik was shaken from his thoughts by his ringtone. It was Bjorn.

'So what have you decided?'

'About what?'

'Are you keeping or dropping loganberry?'

'You win – I'm going to drop it and focus on rolling out plain Oaty.'

'Good call. The reason I called is that I woke up remembering a diagram about roll-outs that we used in class. It's on one of my favourite charts – just like the last one I sent you. I think that this one makes it quite clear what you need to think about and where your potential risks lie. I just sent it to you.'

Erik was too tired to object. He opened his laptop and blinked as the diagram came up.

**Going for growth: roll-out to valuable customers.**

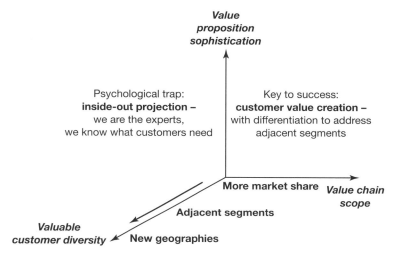

'You see, the psychological trap in roll-out is essentially the same as one of the secrets of successful entrepreneurship: starting with what you have and projecting inside-out on to the market opportunities.'

'I guess that's what makes it difficult for us entrepreneurs to let go once we have an idea that we want to pursue – sometimes we feel like we create the market.'

'Absolutely. That's why you need to remember that roll-out is about creating value for *customers*, giving the market what *it* wants, not getting distracted and diversifying to give it what *you* think it needs. That, of course, doesn't mean you can't innovate, but you need to do it incrementally, like Logitech did. It came up with the mouse, rolled it out and later differentiated it depending on what new customers in adjacent segments asked for. It was only later that it started to design complementary products. It didn't force-feed its customers – like you were trying to do with the loganberry flavour.'

'Drop it, will you?!'

'Oh, and another thing – to roll-out successfully, you need to make sure you have everyone on board and that you have an efficient delivery system. You need to train people and then let *them* take the initiative, because you won't be able to micromanage – you need widespread participation and buy-in for your vision. The entire organization needs to be engaged, which means that you need to support people with facilitation and coaching. Once they're up to speed, let them go for the growth on their own.'

Erik interrupted.

'Actually, I wanted to talk to you about that. I think we need to bring someone on board who could do that. Someone who could engage our teams but also challenge Per and myself. I don't want to make the same mistake twice.'

Bjorn was silent for a couple of seconds.

'I think I know someone who might be just the right person. She has helped me in the past. Her name is Caroline and she runs her own consulting firm. She might be interested. Let me give her a call.'

# Secrets of Going for Growth

The psychological trap is that we think we're the experts, we know what customers want.

Those of us who are entrepreneurs, scientists, researchers, engineers, financial advisers, designers and product developers of all kinds are especially prone to falling into this trap. We are the experts, we understand the ins and outs of our products. We are the only ones who can figure out what will be needed for the roll-out and it's not something that customers can be expected to worry about or comprehend. If we've had one or two winners, then there's little doubt that we know what will work in the next phase of the roll-out. If we haven't helped develop it, it isn't going to work.

Erik was convinced that customers in the oat milk market would want the same kind of variety that he'd seen in the software market. However, the oat milk market was in the very first stages of development. People wanted to try the original genuine thing first, not some modified copy.

At Apple, Steve Jobs has proved to be one of the greatest product development geniuses of all time. He came up with the first really usable personal computer, the blockbuster Apple II. If anybody could sense what would be needed next, he was the one. What was needed next was the Mac, to be followed by the Lisa, with proprietary software to protect it from the copycats. However, customers wanted compatible software and weren't interested in the Lisa. Later, when the Mac roll-out ran out of steam, John Sculley had already caught the Apple bug. He knew that consumers wanted the Apple design and user-friendly software in all their electronic products. However, those markets were full of aggressive competitors. Michael Spindler owed his success to the appeal of the Apple formula in the European market and then saw its erosion in the face of price competition. With the right pricing, he knew Apple was a winner and the formula could be extended into not only consumer electronics but also the office and business market. However, business customers didn't particularly value design.

## Smart Psychology

*Prior to making a big commitment to a roll-out, it's essential that you and your people put yourselves into the shoes of your customers in the new markets.*

Observe their buying and product usage behaviour, ask and find out exactly what they want. Don't talk to your internal experts about the buying behaviour in the new markets. Don't use an internally designed customer satisfaction survey to confirm that they need your existing value proposition without modification as is.

Erik found out the hard way that the market wasn't ready for his loganberry flavour. Steve Jobs had the humiliation of being pushed out of the company he had created. In his subsequent start-ups and new product development at Pixar and NeXT, he learned through trial and error how to align his product creation genius with what customers actually want rather than what he believed customers would want, relying far more on already manifested consumer preferences.

## Smart Strategy

*To justify the focus of resources on roll-out, the market already has to be there and the growth opportunity worth the effort.*

Apart from the potential need for incremental adaptation, the business model should be well tested and already making good money.

At Oaty, it was a matter of getting rid of the dilution of resources and effort caused by the attempt at diversification and focusing instead on the rapidly growing demand for the original product.

At Apple, Sculley stopped the Lisa project, opened up some of the proprietary software for developers and concentrated on the huge PC market for the Mac.

Later on, when he came back to Apple, Jobs also first got rid of distractions such as the Newton and then focused on leveraging Apple's core design capability to roll the iMac out into the loyal consumer market.

After creating the new iTunes and iPod business model, Jobs rolled it out into the market for downloaded music that had already been opened up by Napster and others, and was crying out for a replacement after Napster's departure.

## Smart Risk Management

*For roll-out you have to balance marketing with adequate delivery capability and capacity.*

At Apple, Sculley reorganized and tightened up the organization before rolling out the Mac. The excesses generated by diversification first had to be removed by restructuring, as Amelio and then Jobs actioned, before the roll-out of the iMac would be possible.

*The later stages of roll-out require the development of a complementary capability to differentiate the value proposition for new markets.*

Starting with its core design and user-friendly software, under Jobs's guidance, Apple continually enhanced the unique customer experience that it offers and increase consumer access to it. Jobs clearly wanted to position Apple as the digital hub of not only the home but also wherever people are on the move. Apple acquired and integrated complementary new capabilities into its technology platform in the form of mobile music for the iPod and, most recently, mobile telephony and data services for the iPhone. What made the difference was not the bundling together of existing technologies, but their integration into Apple's existing, superior design and user-friendly software experience. Thus, Apple could introduce dramatically new value propositions while keeping the execution risk to a minimum.

*In terms of leadership, to prevent the roll-out from losing steam after the launch, the frontline organization must remain energized.*

At Oaty, Erik was beginning to face up to the challenge of ensuring that the entire organization was engaged and the frontline staff trained to accelerate the roll-out.

Apple benefited from not only Jobs's product development genius but also his charismatic personality. Exciting products and an exciting leader made Apple one of the best places to work and infused everyone with the extra energy needed to turn a roll-out into an industry blockbuster.

Going for growth is a big move but it carries the least risk as it takes advantage of an already successful business model. The first challenge is to avoid being distracted by other opportunities and to focus energy and resources wholly on the roll-out. The second challenge is to make the necessary adjustments to the value proposition to penetrate new markets. In both instances, it is essential to avoid relying on internal experts and find out exactly what customers want, using that as the basis for customer acquisition and market development.

# 3

# Getting Back into Shape

*Getting back into shape* is about improving the performance of the business by reducing costs and increasing the efficiency of the value chain of activities. It often involves rebalancing the business model after a heavy focus on either the value proposition or valuable customers. This is about correcting error or excess. After finding a new game and paying excessive attention to product development, it may be necessary to get back into shape – as in Wipro's case after the big move into software services. Similarly, this may be needed before or after giving attention to customers, as happened after the roll-out of HSBC's trade financing in the early years (see later in this chapter). Finally, it may be necessary before or after repositioning the value proposition with the acquisition of a new business, as occurred several times in the history of HSBC.

**Getting back into shape.**

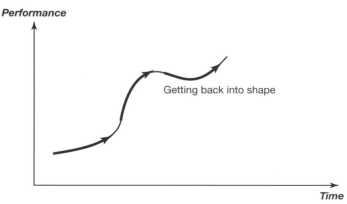

In Erik's story, getting back into shape followed the initial roll-out of the original oat milk product.

The psychological trap in getting back into shape is believing that there's nothing wrong with the business, nothing needs correcting because we are the best (see Beware Narcissistic Denial next – ignoring negative information because we're successful). However, if the business is not put back into shape, it is likely to face brutal restructuring later. So, we have to face the facts, the reality of the deterioration in performance (see HSBC: Not Denial but Reality later in this chapter). To get the business back into shape, the secret is to reduce the execution risk, taking the time to develop the capabilities to support higher volumes, better processes or greater networking efficiency (see Real Realignment near the end of this chapter). Getting back into shape calls for taskforces to re-engineer the value chain and develop the new capability prototypes. Although this needs top-down leadership, the participation of the entire organization is needed later on to change behaviours and embed the capabilities in the organization.

## Beware Narcissistic Denial

Erik, mobile still in hand, strode into Per's lab.

'Per, that was the CEO of Tesco. He's threatening to cancel our contract.'

'What's his problem? Oaty is flying off his shelves. We can hardly keep up with demand.'

'Apparently, some deliveries were late and some stuff landed up in the wrong shops.'

'Erik, he's lucky he's got access to Oaty. We're doing better than we dreamed. We already own 60 per cent of the non-dairy drinks market in Sweden. We're the best-known brand in both Germany and the UK and we're getting great press. Just look at this report on how the market for non-dairy drinks is taking off.'[1]

Per showed Erik the report by Organic Monitor that he had been looking at when Erik walked in.

## Organic Monitor

Home          About Us          Specialist Industries          Industry Watch

**RESEARCH PUBLICATION**

**# 1002-50 THE EUROPEAN MARKET FOR NON-DAIRY DRINKS**

Country Coverage: UK, Germany, Italy, France, Spain
Pricing Scheme:
Full Report  EUR 2,995  (GB £2,065)
Country Chapters  EUR 600  (GB £414)

Published: October 2005
Pages: 237

**Retailers Increase Shelf-Space to Meet Growing Demand for Non-Dairy Drinks**
The growing popularity of non-dairy drinks is responsible for sales to increase by over 20% per annum since the late 1990s.

Initially most consumer demand for non-dairy drinks was from Europeans suffering from lactose intolerance, however demand has broadened in recent years. Non-dairy drinks are increasingly bought as healthy alternatives to dairy milk. Manufacturers are focusing on new product development with new launches including soya juice mixes and fresh soya drinks.

Mainstream retailers account for most non-dairy drink sales with 64% market share. Dairy alternatives are becoming a category in supermarkets with many retailers adding chilled soya drinks and rice drinks to their product ranges. The launch of soya drinks under retailer private labels is causing a large rise in sales volume in the German and British markets. Supermarket private labels account for almost 60% of all soya drink sales in the UK.

The German non-dairy drinks market has overtaken the British market to become the largest in Europe in 2005. High growth is occurring in the German market partly because of discount stores launching non-dairy drinks under their private labels. A number of new entrants have come into the German market since 2001, causing a large rise in domestic production. New entrants have reduced the share of non-dairy drink imports from 82% in 2001 to about a half in 2005.

Erik glanced at the document and back at his friend.

'Per, that's all great, but we've got to do something about our delivery problems. We need to put some time and resources into fixing our logistics.'

'Come on Erik, the Tesco guy probably got out the wrong side of the bed. We've just invested in another plant to meet demand. More cash will be needed for working capital. We have to put everything into getting stuff out the front door. Plus, I have some great products under development and I need the cash to fund the R&D. My guys are on a roll.'

'Have you looked at what's happening to our margins? We've got more breakdowns, more waste, increasing costs.'

'Look, the important thing is that we created this revolutionary product. The only thing that matters to me is that as many people as possible can drink it. It's better than milk, better than soya. It's the best thing since sliced bread. We can't afford to slow down. The few glitches we have are growth problems that'll sort themselves out with time.'

'Per, the least we need to do is fix the problem with Tesco. Do you realize how much work I put into getting that Tesco contract for us? Their request for on-time delivery at multiple locations is not something our current platform can deliver. If we lose Tesco, we lose our growth momentum.'

Caroline walked into the room as Per responded heatedly.

'I'm not sure about that. There are lots of other customers out there. Wasn't the Polish production company you encouraged us to buy supposed to ease this kind of thing?'

Erik sat down heavily. To become the preferred supplier to Tesco was a huge challenge for the company. He felt let down by his childhood friend.

Caroline looked at the two men. She could not have dreamt of a better moment to intervene.

'Gentlemen, congratulations – I saw the article on Oaty in *Svenska Dagensblatt*. You're doing well.

The two men looked at each other, momentarily taken off balance. Getting up, Per smiled. Maybe hiring this consultant wasn't a bad idea after all. He thanked her as he left. He was running late for a meeting with his chief scientist.

Caroline turned to Erik.

'Would you like to share the problem with me?'

'Well, actually, I seem to have run into a dead-end with Per. He's so proud of how well his brainchild product has done that he can't see we don't have what it takes for the next step. Yes, he invented oat milk, but what's a great product worth if we can't deliver it on time to the big retail chains? We have real problems with our logistics that he refuses to accept. I've tried to discuss the issue with him but we clearly don't see eye to eye.'

'Per wouldn't be the first scientist, nor the first businessman, to believe that his business has done so well that there can't be anything really wrong with it. The classic symptoms are a refusal to accept negative news, especially when success is clear and people repeatedly tell you how great you are. It's called narcissistic denial.'

'Per is anything but narcissistic.'

'It happens to all of us. You look into the reflecting pool of your success and you lose sight of reality. The best way to work this through with Per is to give him facts, something his scientific mind can work with. Give him the brutal facts – a scenario of where this might be heading if no action is taken to correct the balance.'

She continued.

'What the two of you have done so far is focus on innovation and, after your first flop with product diversification, on customer intimacy. It's your focus on customer intimacy that got you the Tesco deal. You knew what your customer was after and you delivered excellent service, but you've lost sight of efficiency – that's what you're telling me. You think it's time to invest in new logistics, so your operations will be aligned for delivery to large retailers, but Per doesn't see the need. If you talk to Per in terms of future scenarios, he might get your point. Let's sit down and find a way of sharing your view with Per that he can relate to. Realignment calls for a top-down approach, one that you will both need to back, especially if you are going to take resources away from one part of the organization to commit them to another part.'

The next morning, Erik went straight to see Per. His friend was sitting at his computer, coffee in hand.

'Listen, Per, I'm sorry about my reaction yesterday. We need to find a way to make this work. This Tesco deal is huge for us.'

'It's fine. Look at this – I'm working on an oat-based batter. That way we can make oat milk pancakes.'

'That's great – another innovation from Oaty Lab! I had a good discussion with Caroline after you left. She also suggested that I speak with Bjorn, so I met up with him yesterday afternoon.'

Per looked at Erik suspiciously.

'And?'

Erik looked almost embarrassed.

'It's just that … he thought you might find this interesting.'

Per glanced at the papers in Erik's hands.

'Bjorn thought I would find *banking* interesting?'

'Listen, just look through it when you need a break. He made some notes and I made a few myself. Just think about it, OK?'

## HSBC: Not Denial but Reality

---

**HSBC**

*Note: Emergence of a global financial institution through growth mainly by acquisition. As a result, periodically, the company has recognized that its operations are not integrated and aligned. Management has responded with big moves aimed at increasing efficiency and lowering costs.*

**Going for growth in the early years: roll-out of trade financing**

In 1865, Scotsman Thomas Sutherland founded the Hongkong and Shanghai Banking Corporation. The bank financed and promoted British imperial trade in opium, silk and tea in East Asia and, until the early twentieth century, it operated primarily in Asia and India, opening offices in Europe or the United States as trade dictated.

---

*Getting back into shape: smart big move – realigning the organization by developing international managers to integrate far-flung geographic operations*

To integrate its spread-out network of offices, HSBC developed a cadre of 250 young officers, known as international managers or IMs. These IMs – primarily British and London-trained – were committed to an expatriate career as troubleshooters. They could not choose their assignment location and, until recently, they could not marry and remain IMs without their boss's approval.

Over time, these young bankers grew to become country heads, originally in Asia and then across the company's operations worldwide. The IMs represented the essence of HSBC's culture – the glue that held the organization together and allowed the exchange of best internal practice.

*Going for growth: 1950–1980 roll-out of acquisition strategy, leveraging the balance sheet to acquire distressed undercapitalized banks*

HSBC played an important role in the growth of Hong Kong after World War II by financing industrialists who fled China. From the 1950s to the 1970s, HSBC expanded aggressively through acquisitions, including the British Bank of the Middle East (now the Saudi British Bank). In 1962, HSBC bought a controlling stake in Hang Seng, Hong Kong's largest bank – the first time it acquired a bank not to expand its geographical reach but rather to take out a competitor.

Throughout the 1970s, HSBC bought a number of smaller European banks. These subsidiaries were locally incorporated and their capital was locally domiciled. In the late 1970s, as China began to welcome foreign business, HSBC opened offices in North America to capitalize on the business between the United States, China and Canada.

*Failure to relaunch growth in the USA: Sandberg's early 1980s stupid big move – acquiring and accepting Marine Midland's view that there was nothing wrong with its management*

In 1980, under Chairman Michael Sandberg, to access the world's reserve currency and diversify away from Hong Kong, HSBC bought a controlling stake in the struggling Buffalo, New York-based Marine Midland Bank.

HSBC agreed to retain Marine Midland's entire senior management team – a concession that made change difficult to execute. At one point, HSBC had lost roughly a third of its investment and so Sandberg sent in an IM, Keith Whitson, to turn the situation around. He streamlined management, refurbished the branches and implemented new customer-friendly service offerings. By 1994, Midland was profitable again.

Following the 1984 agreement to return Hong Kong to China, Sandberg decided to increase HSBC's UK presence. He bought a number of securities operations and smaller banks, opened new operations in Beijing and Guangzhou, bought a bank in Malaysia and added new European branches. By 1987, HSBC had acquired the remaining 49 per cent of Marine Midland, doubling its asset base in the United States. However, it was 1994 before Marine Midland was profitable again.

***Relaunching growth: Purves's 1992–1993 smart big move – acquiring and integrating Midland Bank in the United Kingdom***

In 1992, under Sandberg's successor, William Purves, HSBC acquired Midland Bank (no relation to Marine Midland). Learning from the earlier acquisition in the USA, Purves immediately placed HSBC executives, under the leadership of John Bond, in the top ranks of Midland. The acquisition of Midland dramatically increased HSBC's presence in Europe as a whole by doubling its assets there, spurring HSBC's emergence as a global financial-services company.

Purves made further acquisitions, including banks in Argentina, Brazil and Mexico. HSBC also moved into private banking in the United States with the purchase of Republic Bank and Safra Holdings.

***Getting back into shape: Purves' 1993–1996 smart big move – introducing business lines to realign the organization and improve efficiency***

In preparation for Hong Kong's return to China, HSBC reorganized as a holding in 1991 and, two years later, relocated its headquarters, moving from Hong Kong to London. Its subsidiaries remained independent, however, responsible separately for their balance sheets – head office simply provided guidance in terms of strategic planning, HR, legal counsel, administrative aid and financial planning and control.

Recognizing that HSBC was reaching the limits of decentralization, Purves set out to reorganize the bank into a matrix structure. In addition to the country organization, he introduced customer groups, or lines of business.[2] These groups were given titles and included Corporate and Investment Banking and Markets, Personal Financial Services, Private Banking, and Commercial and Merchant Banking. To facilitate decision making in the matrix, customer group heads often also served as regional heads.

***Getting back into shape: Bond's 1996–2000 smart big move – realigning the organization by managing for value, improving financial efficiency with value-based management***

John Bond – who had successfully turned Midland Bank around – became HSBC's first CEO under Purves in 1993. Three years later, he replaced Purves as Chairman. Bond appointed Keith Whitson – who had turned Marine Midland around – as CEO.

Bond's ambitions for the bank were big. He wanted HSBC to become the most profitable bank of its peer group, overtake Citigroup by the time the bank moved into its new London headquarters, double shareholder return by 2003 and balance earnings equally between developed and developing countries.

The financial community was less optimistic, however. It undervalued the bank, believing that its full potential as a global group was as yet unrealized. In the late 1990s, most of the company's earnings were still generated in Hong Kong and Britain – mature markets with little potential for growth. Also, 95 per cent of the group's profits came from 5 economies, only 1 per cent from India and Latin America, yet about half of the group's assets were in the developing world, making it vulnerable to crises in those regions.

Bond introduced a 'Managing for Value' strategy, aiming for a higher return on equity. He introduced metrics for a much stronger focus on cost control and, especially, an efficient use of capital and greater return on assets.

Bond decided to increase the focus on asset management and private banking because the capital needed was lower. In two years, HSBC went from $75 billion of funds under management to around $270 billion.

**Failure to relaunch growth: Bond's 2000–2003 big stupid move – acquiring and then accepting that there was nothing wrong with Crédit Commercial de France and Household consumer finance**

In 2000, HSBC acquired Crédit Commercial de France (CCF, with 30,000 private banking clients and 10 per cent of the French private banking market) and the Republic National Bank of New York (with 30,000 high net worth individuals in Switzerland, France, Luxembourg, Guernsey, Gibraltar and Monaco). These acquisitions made HSBC one of the top competitors in private banking and greatly strengthened its position in the Euro Zone.

In 2001, it acquired Barclays Bank's fund management operations in Greece.

Some of those moves were not smart. The acquisition of CCF was criticized because it departed from the bank's tradition of buyouts of distressed companies. HSBC paid 2.5 times the book value for CCF, which had cost ratios that were way out of line, then left the management of CCF intact.

By the end of 2001, HSBC had spent over $21 billion on acquisitions and new ventures and made another 27 acquisitions between January 2002 and September 2003. These were more traditional acquisitions of weaker banks, including purchases in Turkey, Mexico and Shanghai.

In March 2003, HSBC expanded its consumer finance operations by purchasing US-based Household International (now known as HSBC Finance). The $14 billion acquisition helped transform HSBC into one of the world's biggest financial institutions. Household's $98 billion in assets and 53 million accounts gave HSBC immediate access to a large retail market. It meant that the group could now book 30 per cent of its pre-tax earnings in North America, 32 per cent in Europe and 37 per cent in Asia.[3] It reflected Bond's ambition to make HSBC the 'world's local bank'.

The move was not smart, however. Household was a high-risk operation that was still under scrutiny regarding allegations of predatory lending policies and the acquisition tripled HSBC's provisions for bad or doubtful debts. Experts wondered if HSBC had the expertise needed to succeed in the subprime market. HSBC responded that this was precisely why it had acquired Household – not only to extend its reach in the USA but also to gain access to the statistical credit risk models designed by the company's cadre of 150 PhDs. As HSBC had no other operations and senior executives with this type of credit risk experience, it left most of Household's top management in place.

For the first 3 years of the market's recovery, Household averaged a return on investment for HSBC of around 17 per cent. Then, in the third quarter of 2006, Household's mortgage books showed significant losses and HSBC shares dropped by 9 per cent. The bank reacted by putting in place much tougher measures in the United States and pulling out from second lien mortgages.

### Going for growth: Green's 2003–2006 smart big move – shifting away from acquisitions and rolling out organic growth based on increased cross-selling

Stephen Green, a former McKinsey consultant who had spent 24 years with the bank, became CEO at the time of the Household acquisition. Green led a strategic shift away from acquisitions as the major vehicle for growth and towards growing the company organically with a new strategy called 'Managing for Growth'.

The new strategy called for capitalizing on HSBC's global footprint to roll out its value propositions around the world, especially in emerging markets. The strategy was evolutionary rather than revolutionary, building on the company's strengths, including its consumer finance products.

Green wanted the divisions to work more closely together, serving the bank's most profitable customers. The key business objectives were to accelerate the rate of growth of revenue, develop the brand strategy further, improve productivity and maintain the group's prudent risk management and strong financial position.[4]

▶

***Getting back into shape: Geoghegan's 2006–2007 smart big move – realigning the bank with shared best practices to increase global efficiency***

After eight years as Chairman, Bond stepped down in May 2006. Green replaced him as Chairman and Michael Geoghegan took over as CEO.

Geoghegan realized that reducing the reliance on acquisitions was not enough. The bank was too dispersed. Cross-selling couldn't reach its full potential without much tighter integration and cost control.

This flaw became especially transparent in 2007, when the sub-prime crisis began to hit Household with full force. HSBC was forced to make larger and larger credit losses. Traditional HSBC bankers, including international managers, were sent in to restructure Household and finally integrate it into the US bank and into Personal Financial Services worldwide. HSBC's ability to manage and absorb these problems is manifest in its results: in the first half of 2007, operating income was up 23 per cent to $42 billion and pre-tax profits up 13 per cent to $14.2 billion.

To accelerate global integration, Geoghegan introduced the 'Seven Pillars' strategy, which was designed to complement and support Green's 'Managing for Growth' by sharing the bank's best practices from around the world:[5]

- Our customers – service excellence.

- Our brand – the world's local bank.

- Our culture – the best place to work.

- Our global distribution – our global advantage.

- Our businesses – building for sustained growth.

- Our technology and process – joining up the company.

- Our organization – guidance with wisdom and delegation with confidence.

# Real Realignment

Per put the case study down. He almost hadn't read past the headline; the idea that the oat milk business could learn from big banking seemed too far-fetched. Unlike Erik, he wasn't intrigued by Bjorn's MBA mumbo-jumbo, but the introductory note made him want to read on. HSBC's story of continual growth through acquisition, followed by the need to face reality and periodically rebalance the business model with big moves aimed at increasing efficiency and lowering costs, was clearly Erik's way of trying to get him to reconsider his doubts around the importance of redesigning the company's logistics. Yet, when he reached the end of the case, he wondered: had growth in their Oaty business created the same need for 'getting back into shape', or was Erik simply seduced by Bjorn's MBA stuff?

At the same time, Per couldn't help but feel angry. The logistics problems were mainly coming from the weak link between the Polish factory and the rest of the organization. He hadn't been in favour of acquiring the Polish oat-producing company, which Erik had pushed through last spring, thereby increasing their debt. Yes, Poland was another of Europe's big oat-producing countries and, yes, the factory that came with the acquisition had helped Oaty fulfil the demands of its customers, but he didn't want to disrupt his team by trying to work with outsiders. No attempts were made to integrate the new subsidiary and they just used it to ramp up production. As a result, they had failed to use it to help them with Tesco.

Now, though, he started wondering. Should they have better integrated the Polish company rather than leave it alone as he had wanted? Had it been something too big for them at that point in their growth? Were they off balance?

On the back of the case study, Per found handwritten notes:

> When the value chain is no longer aligned and performance deteriorates, the narcissistic CEO rationalizes away reasons for decline, blaming it on temporary external factors that will go away or minor errors in execution that have already been corrected. When the profit decline persists, new reasons are brought forward to explain away what is happening. When people challenge this narrative, the CEO becomes dismissive, arrogant, even hostile, accusing the critics of defeatism.

**Why do talented people fall into this psychological trap?**

- Grandiose sense of self-importance.

- Fantasies of unlimited success.

- Believe they are special and unique.

- Thrive on excessive admiration.

- Strong sense of entitlement.

- Lack empathy.

- Easily take advantage of others.

**Avoiding narcissistic denial**

- Become more self-reflective. Try to understand your motivation and deeper psychological drivers. Not easy, because may undermine fragile self-confidence.

- Everybody needs a boss. Use Board members as check and balance, as sparring partners.

- Pay attention to appropriate organizational structure and processes, especially your team – don't short-circuit them in pursuit of personal goals.

- Accept wide open dialogue, be willing to learn. When was the last time you and your team put the brutal facts on the table?

From Per's point of view, Erik could hardly have been more direct. Were these Erik's notes or Bjorn's? Per called Bjorn.

'Bjorn, the handwritten notes on the back of the HSBC case study you gave Erik – are those your notes or Erik's?'

'Mine. Why?'

'Well, Erik is obviously trying to send me a message and it'd be even more distasteful if those were his notes, written explicitly to influence me.'

'No, no, they're notes from my MBA days. Do you think that I may be able to help?'

'I have to say, as a scientist, I find the MBA stuff a bit like pop psychology. But I want our business to be the best, so …'

Per took a deep breath.

'I need to understand why you think the HSBC story is relevant for us.'

Per and Bjorn met at a restaurant Erik was unlikely to go to. Per put the case study on the table between them and leaned forward.

'Tell me, how can you possibly compare oat milk and banking? No two technologies could be further apart.'

'That's the point. Leadership isn't about technology. It's about people and human psychology, which hasn't changed much in the last 10,000 years. Yes, the technology – especially in fields such as communications – has changed dramatically, which allows us to organize in different ways. In fact, the main difference between industries is the speed at which the industry-specific technology is evolving, but the essentials of people's behaviour, not the fads, are the same as they were yesterday. As a result, there are patterns that recur across industries. For example, start-ups focus on product development and grow haphazardly as customers find them and spread the word. In the process, the new companies don't give much attention to efficiency and processes. If they then make an acquisition that's not integrated, the problem is compounded.'

Per leaned back.

'Come on, you have a very simplistic view of what we've done.'

Bjorn continued.

'It's a question of opportunities and resources and focusing people. At any point in time, the opportunities are different for innovation, customer orientation and efficiency. You've got to put what are always limited resources behind the best opportunity. Then you need a clear focus for your people. Over time, all companies tend to shift emphasis from one part of the business model to the other. To avoid turning these shifts into big bets, periodically they have to take the time to get back into shape. Oaty has now reached one of those points. There's no doubt that you have to improve your logistics if you want to capitalize on the market opportunity and move Oaty to the next level. Caroline is the right person to help you do that.'

Per didn't say anything. Bjorn pulled out the page from the case that had a chart of HSBC's trajectory over time and made the following notes underneath it:

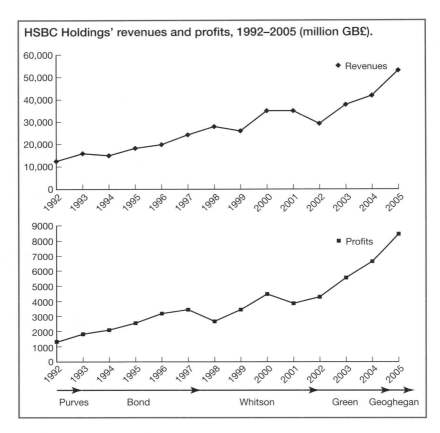

HSBC Holdings' revenues and profits, 1992–2005 (million GB£).

## HSBC's phases of development

**Early years** *Going for growth* with roll-out of trade financing.

**Early years** *Getting back into shape* – smart big move of developing international managers to integrate the organization.

**1950–1980** *Going for growth* with roll-out of acquisition strategy.

**1980–1987** *Failure to relaunch growth* – stupid big move of acquiring and not integrating the Marine Midland acquisition.

**1992–1993** *Relaunching growth* – smart big move of acquiring and integrating Midland Bank.

**1993–1996** *Getting back into shape* – smart big move of introducing business lines to realign the organization with the market.

**1996–2000** *Getting back into shape – smart big move of 'Managing for Value' strategy to achieve alignment and improve financial efficiency.*

**2000–2003** *Failure to relaunch growth – stupid big move of acquiring and then accepting that there was nothing wrong with CCF and Household.*

**2003–2006** *Going for growth – smart big move of shifting away from acquisitions and rolling out organic growth based on increased cross-selling.*

**2006–2007** *Getting back into shape – smart big move of realigning the bank with shared best practices to increase global efficiency.*

Bjorn put down his pen and commented:

'After periods of relaunching growth and/or going for growth, HSBC's leaders realized that they had to get the organization back into shape by introducing international managers in the early years, business lines in 1993, 'Managing for Value' in 1996 and the 'Seven Pillars' in 2007. As with any company, there were stupid moves, such as not integrating the big acquisitions of Marine Midland and Household until profits dropped. Also, HSBC was hit by periodic turbulence in the financial markets: the world wars, collapse of the Hong Kong market in 1997, the Latin American market in 2001, the subprime crisis in 2007. HSBC's leaders, though, always faced reality in time to correct the situation.'

Per interrupted.

'It's not as though there was a strict alternation between growth and getting back into shape.'

'Obviously not in such a large firm, but, even in a huge financial conglomerate, there's a clear periodic need to shift the emphasis back on to costs and efficiency.'

Per fell silent again. The conversation shifted and Bjorn rose to leave. By the time Per got back to the lab, Bjorn had already sent him one of his now familiar diagrams.

**Getting back into shape: realign the value chain.**

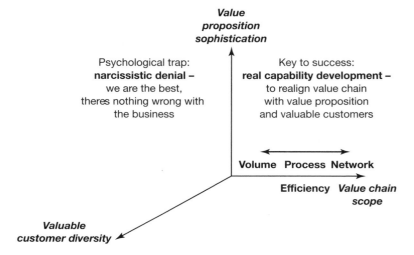

Per could see from the diagram that there were three types of realignment. The first of these was volume efficiency, the second was process efficiency, and the third was network efficiency. He read Bjorn's e-mail:

Once value propositions in the marketplace converge, the stage is set for *volume efficiency* based on standardization and, where appropriate, mass production.

Later on, there may be opportunities for streamlining operations with reorganization (the business lines at HSBC, for example) and *process efficiency*, obtained by re-engineering activities and continuous improvement (classical examples include Kaizen, Six Sigma and the 'Managing for Value' strategy at HSBC).

Finally, in the presence of a variety of value propositions serving different markets, there may be opportunities for *network efficiency*, by optimizing the coordination of partners and

> activities in different value chains using outsourcing, in-house expertise centres and production platforms (the 'Seven Pillars' strategy at HSBC, for instance).
>
> When companies don't realign their value chain, they expose themselves to high risk when they make their next big innovation or customer move.

Per stopped reading. He was reluctant to admit it, but maybe Bjorn and Erik had a point. Maybe there had to be more to their success than excellent R&D. Using the chart, he drew what he saw as Oaty's profile.

**Oaty's business model profile.**

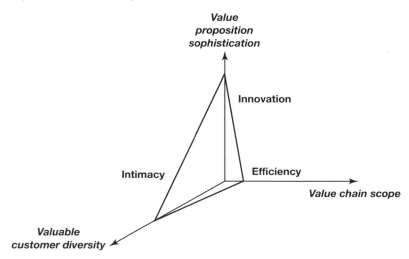

The profile supported what Bjorn, Caroline and Erik had been saying: high on innovation, OK on customer intimacy and low on efficiency. Was there no other solution? Did they have to 're-engineer their value chain', as Bjorn had said? Use taskforces to assess their current situation and determine what needed to be done?

Per disliked taskforces and the like almost as much as he disliked meetings. He could already see more consultants coming in to train them and run seminars on process efficiency. Then again, he had been impressed by Caroline so far. She had the ability to get people to work together in a focused way on common problems across organizational boundaries. If *she* led their effort to improve logistics, he could see it happening in a productive way with the minimum of wasted time.

## Secrets of Getting Back into Shape

The psychological trap is that we think we're the best, we're successful and there is nothing wrong with the business.

It's often difficult to see whether a drop in bottom-line performance is temporary and will be self-correcting or is the sign of declining efficiency and competitiveness. You cannot change course for every bump in the road or react to every critic out there. You have to keep the business on track. One of the reasons you've been successful is that you know how to deal with adversity and stay the course. So, the natural inclination is to develop a thick skin and ignore weak negative signals. You have to deal firmly with the purveyors of doom and gloom. To maintain the energy of your people, you have to shield them from the distractions and remind them how well you've all done, saying, 'We're successful and among the best, there's nothing fundamentally wrong with our business.'

At Oaty, Per had created the product and seen the market improve and grow and the media respond. The business formula they had was clearly working. They had to keep their eye on the ball, get the product out of the door and look at adaptations for adjacent markets. If Tesco didn't want to play ball, he felt that was their problem.

When HSBC acquired Marine Midland, CCF and then Household, all three acquired managements believed there was nothing fundamentally wrong with their business models – their view was that HSBC was just lucky to acquire them as they passed through a rough patch. For its part, HSBC so much wanted the presence in the USA and continental Europe, and then a greater presence in the USA, that keeping the management in place seemed a more than reasonable price to pay. After all, HSBC's top management had made so many successful acquisitions that they could handle it. The mainly external critics could be brushed off. They didn't see the full picture.

## Smart Psychology

*To get back into shape, the smart psychology is to check your views of the business trajectory with the views of different people on the front line and face the brutal facts.*

For example, if you've been through a long growth spurt or made many acquisitions, chances are that the organization is dispersed and possibly fragmented, so it will need to get back into shape.

At Oaty, the growth shift to larger customers had uncovered the weakness in logistics. Per had the advantage of being gently coached by Bjorn, Erik and Caroline on the need to get things back into shape and he had the good sense to listen and eventually see the logic of their position.

At HSBC, the executives on both sides of the fateful acquisitions succumbed to believing that there was nothing wrong with the deals, despite the fact that they broke with HSBC's proven acquisition success formula of taking over only distressed banks and sending in trusted managers to turn them around. However, once bad results proved the deals were defective, HSBC saw this and was very good at sending seasoned executives in to clean things up.

## Smart Strategy

*The strategic secret to successful realignment is getting costs under control with better volume, process or network efficiency and aiming for a competitive edge in the value chain activities.*

At Oaty, they were about to put in place much improved logistics so that the firm could deliver in a reliable and cost-effective way to large accounts such as Tesco.

At HSBC, top management recognized the need to consolidate and integrate the organization after periods of acquisition-driven growth in order to reap the benefits of its larger size and avoid being submerged by it. The most recent big move to get back into shape and create one bank with the 'Seven Pillars' strategy, if successful, would give HSBC the opportunity to cross-sell financial services on a global scale that few could match.

## Smart Risk Management

*The biggest risk of imbalance during realignment is that product innovation and/or customer intimacy are so dominant that realignment doesn't take root.*

The emphasis on growth at both Oaty and HSBC was such that the realignment might not be deep enough to get the business back into shape. At HSBC in the 1990s, one round of realignment was not enough. The introduction of business lines between 1993 and 1996 helped to tilt the balance from customer geography towards global product segments. In addition, it required the 'Managing for Value' strategy from 1996 to 2000 to reduce costs and improve financial efficiency, then, in the mid-2000s, the 'Seven Pillars' strategy to integrate the organization.

*The complementarity challenge in getting back into shape is to sequence the development of efficiency capabilities so that they build on one another.*

It is impossible, for example, to develop the network efficiency of the organization without effective processes that tie the organization together. Further, processes can't be installed without some stability in the operating technology provided by volume-efficient production.

At HSBC, the back office, high-volume transaction activity was outsourced. Seamless processes were then needed to feed the products produced by these platforms to the point of customer contact where they could be pulled together into a customized value proposition. Thereafter, to make cross-selling work, organizational integration became a must.

*The implementation risk in getting back into shape is that the new capabilities are not properly piloted in taskforces and the behaviours don't change on the front line.*

Successful execution calls for a chairman-type leadership style to orchestrate the taskforce process, followed by the kind of organizational coaching that Caroline was brought in to provide at Oaty to facilitate a change in behaviour on the front line. By contrast, HSBC was such a large organization, comprising acquired cultures added over many years, that it would have resisted the more measured chairman and organizational coaching styles. Mike Geoghegan's commander style probably was the best guarantee that behaviours actually would change to create a globally integrated bank.

Getting back into shape and improving efficiency is not that exciting and the need is often more diffuse than for the other big moves. Apart from not being willing to accept that there is anything wrong, the biggest risk is declining commitment and lack of completion. Making the organization follow through on execution and not allowing other priorities to get in the way is essential. Taking the time to really get the value chain of activities back into shape is frequently a secret to the success of the next big move.

Relaunching
Growth

"We can beat any
competitor"

# 4

# Relaunching Growth

*Relaunching growth* is about avoiding declining revenues by repositioning the value proposition in a distinctive way relative to the existing competition. It's about developing or acquiring a new value proposition for a specific target market. Depending on the circumstances, relaunching growth can come into play after any of the other strategic moves. Growth may have to be relaunched after it runs out of steam due to market saturation or increasing competition or it may be needed after getting back into shape or restoring profitability. At HSBC, with the ambition to be one of the largest global financial service firms, relaunching growth came into play repeatedly after losing momentum in going for growth and after getting back into shape. At Dow Corning, as we shall see, it was the big move after coming out of bankruptcy. At Oaty, relaunching growth was the next big move after getting back into shape.

**Relaunching growth.**

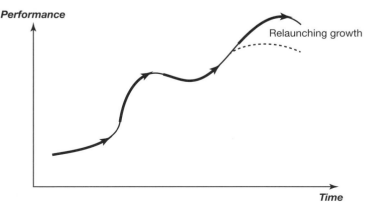

The common psychological trap in relaunching growth is that of copying the fastest-growing competitor and believing you can beat them at their own game (see Beware 'Me Too' Imitation next – believing that copying the herd will revitalize growth). Success in relaunching growth comes not from copying the fastest-growing competitor, but from differentiation and being distinctive from the competition (see Dow Corning: Not Imitation but Distinctiveness later in this chapter). To reduce the risk of failing with the implementation, it's important to target the development of the new value proposition at a specific market segment (see Distinctive Repositioning near the end of this chapter). In terms of execution, creative pilot projects are needed to test new value propositions in the targeted market segments and new capabilities have to be developed to ensure effective delivery.

# Beware 'Me Too' Imitation

Caroline took the lead when it came to putting in the new logistics processes, as well as organizing the training and coaching needed to develop the right behaviours for customer-focused, speedy delivery. She turned the Polish operations around so effectively that Erik and Per offered Caroline the job of COO. She was so involved with Oaty, she accepted.

The 18 months since then, however, took their toll emotionally. Developing an effective logistics capability for the whole company took much longer than either Erik or Per imagined. The arguments between the two men over the impact of process re-engineering on the company's culture strained their friendship. In spite of Caroline's efforts, employees picked up on the tension and Oaty's CFO left, complaining that he couldn't get Per and Erik to agree on whether the priority was growth or processes. Oaty lost a large retailer in Germany when it failed to get its logistics organized in time to meet the retailer's on-time delivery requirements. Most worrying of all, revenues had stopped growing. In recent months, the dairy industry had retaliated with a 95 per cent lactose-free product that was eating into their market and their margins.

As he walked out of the office, Erik realized how much he was looking forward to his long weekend in London with Viveka. He needed the break.

Viveka had reluctantly agreed that they would spend the first morning looking around retailers, checking out the offering in the London market. The United Kingdom was the most developed market in organic and non-dairy food and drinks. On Friday morning, the couple walked through Tesco, Sainsbury's, healthfood shops and Harvey Nichols. As they walked back into the reception of their hotel, Erik's BlackBerry beeped. It was a message from Per.

> Just got a press release: the Redwood Co. is launching a line of dairy-free cheeses, called Cheezly: feta style in oil, meltable nacho style, and grated Cheddar-style. They're made from soya, starch and non-hydrogenated vegetable fats – completely free of animal products. Low in fat, too. They're putting Cheezly in healthfood shops and Sainsbury's.[1]

Erik called Per.

'Your message and what I've just seen are about to destroy my weekend. There are *dozens* of competing products out here. I found the Lactolite milk, but I also found a lactose-free brand of margarine called Pure and, listen to this: part of their sales pitch is that it's free of soy, gluten, wheat – and *oats*, as if oats were something to be *wary* of! We need to be doing what these guys are doing – our current offering isn't enough to compete with all these new segments. Our competitors have diversified far more than we have. We need to beat them at this variety game.'

Per tried reassuring Erik.

'Erik, we're almost there with the pancake dough and we're pushing ahead with the ice-cream.'

Erik said goodbye and hung up. They had been so focused on their internal issues that they'd given their competitors an easy ride. Now that they had put in place state-of-the-art logistics, they needed to go back to focusing on their product development.

There was nothing Erik could do about all of this right then, so he joined Viveka at a fashion show by an up-and-coming London designer.

☆ ☆ ☆

Back in Malmö, Erik, Per and Caroline invited Bjorn to lunch. They needed a fresh perspective. Bjorn opened by teasing Erik.

'Are you *sure* you don't want to do an MBA? In the end, it might be less expensive than my consulting fees.'

'As long as the price of beer doesn't go up, we'll manage your fees.'

Erik was more tolerant of Bjorn's kidding ever since Bjorn had worked with Caroline to bring Per round to understanding the importance of their logistics needs and to integrate their Polish operations. Becoming more serious, Bjorn continued.

'So, looks like the competition has caught up with you.'

'You can say that again. There are many good products out there. We need to think carefully about how to deal with this growing diversity of both products and competitors.'

Per chipped in.

'Most of those products are not half as good as ours. Who wants to put soya milk into their morning coffee? It's like having beans for breakfast and, besides, I have a *dozen* great products in the pipeline.'

'True,' replied Caroline, 'but soya milk still owns 90 per cent of a world market worth $2 billion.'

'Now that our logistics are in shape, we'll start catching up. Did you see the recent life cycle analysis? Oaty generates a far smaller quantity of greenhouse gases per unit than dairy milk and uses a quarter of the acreage. Our carbon footprint is much smaller. Those things count today! Other products can't make that claim. Also, some of them are bound to be slowed down by the same types of growing pains that we hit.'

'So what are you going to do?' Bjorn asked.

Per's voice grew confident.

'We're going to be number one in product diversity. We're going to beat all these Johnny-come-lately guys. Anything they do, we can do better. Right now I have a new strawberry flavour, ready-made pancake dough, vanilla custard – specifically for the British market – and, the latest thing, a kiwi and green tea flavoured drink.'

'So what's the problem? You guys don't need me.'

Erik looked at his old friend.

'Well, despite the promising new products, our Nordic and European sales aren't really growing. If this were the IT industry, we would have 10 times the revenue by now and we'd be looking for an industry giant to buy us, but, in this industry, when you come up with new products, the competitors start cutting prices. We need to think carefully about our next steps.'

'Would you care for another case study?'

Caroline smiled.

'Why do you think we invited you to lunch?!'

## Dow Corning: Not Imitation but Distinctiveness

### Dow Corning

Founded in 1943 in the USA, Dow Corning is owned jointly by Dow Chemical and Corning Inc., formerly Corning Glass Works. Corning had researched potential commercial applications for silicone as early as the 1930s, but it needed a chemical industry partner to help it manufacture the product. Dow Corning's first success was a silicone seal that ensured that the Allied forces' World War II fighter planes' ignitions did not fail at high altitudes.

*Going for growth: 1950–1990 rolling out innovative new products*

After the war, the company started looking at non-military applications for the product and found plenty. Dow Corning created more than 5000 products, driving growth during the 1950s and 1960s.

Dow Corning's researchers also looked into the effects of silicone on organisms and the environment. They found silicone to be an inert product with no evident side-effects, making it ideal for medical applications, such as in pacemakers or as coating on needles. In 1959, the company opened the Center for Aid to Medical Research to support in-house and independent research on silicone. Five years later, it produced the first silicone breast implant for women who had suffered mastectomies. The product was soon used in both reconstructive and cosmetic surgery, and Dow Corning became the leader in both markets.

The company grew rapidly between the 1960s and 1990s, remaining the market leader in the increasingly competitive implants market and introducing significant product innovations in 1974 and 1979. Recognizing its pioneering role – and its in-depth product testing – the medical industry trusted Dow Corning (between 1970 and 1990, the company was taken to court only twice).

Its luck ran out in 1989, however, when the company launched what would be the last implant it would market. In December 1991, Dow Corning lost a $7.3 million breast implant. Four months later, it left the implant market altogether. Competitors had no chance to take advantage: Bristol-Myers Squibb and 3M were also losing lawsuits. In March 1994, the implant manufacturers accepted the largest ever mass tort settlement in history, involving 410,000 claims. Fourteen months later, Dow Corning filed for bankruptcy.

***Failure to relaunch growth: 1997–2000 stupid big move – reorganization of the existing product portfolio around end-user segments without distinctive innovation***

On 25 August 1997, Dow Corning announced a reorganization plan. It would focus on end-user segments, such as construction, healthcare and electronics, and proactively resolve the outstanding breast implant claims. However, the proposed business model was based on Dow Corning's existing portfolio of products without any distinctive innovation.

Revenues remained flat after the reorganization. Most of the company's clients were companies in emerging markets or markets experiencing rapid technological change (everything from microelectronics manufacturers to skincare companies) and they were defecting in large numbers to low-cost suppliers no longer willing to pay Dow Corning's premium prices.

Competition came from two sides: large companies with efficient supply chains that gave them economies of scale and small local players that eschewed R&D in favour of low-end, bulk silicone products at very low prices. A number of silicone products had become commodities over time (for example, those sold through DIY shops and for pulp and paper processing). Differentiation was difficult to achieve. Profit margins for many of the more mature products had been declining for several years.

*Failure to relaunch growth: Hazleton's 2000–2001 stupid big
move – cutting costs and prices to try and beat competitors at
their own game*

Dow Corning failed to see the signs of the industry's increasing
commoditization and made no move to refashion the old business
model that had made it successful. In the managers' minds, the
company's products still demanded a premium.

Between 1999 and 2000, sales sank by nearly 11 per cent and, in
2001, under Chairman Richard Hazleton, Dow Corning experienced
its fifth consecutive year of stagnating revenues. Cost-cutting and
layoffs to match the competition helped, but nowhere near enough.
Finally, management recognized that the company needed to completely revisit its business model. Cornered, Dow Corning radically
changed its strategy.

*Relaunching growth: Anderson's 2001–2003 smart big move –
repositioning with new segmentation and a distinctive new
brand for the low end market, plus tailored propositions for the
other segments*

In March 2001, CEO Gary Anderson was elected Chairman and
challenged Dow Corning's cadre of middle managers to come up
with BHAGs (big, hairy, audacious goals). To drive home the importance of the initiative, the company put its best people – its future
leaders – on the teams. The teams spent three months looking at
the company's past, present and future.

The taskforces came back with two main conclusions. First, some
of the company's products were indeed commodities for which no
one was willing to pay a premium price – Dow Corning's extra service offerings notwithstanding. This was particularly true in
construction materials. Second, the taskforces found that innovation mattered more in healthcare and electronics. Customers in
those industries *were* willing to pay for additional services.

The self-audit teams found, however, that, even for its most loyal
customers, Dow Corning's high prices outweighed its track record
as a premium company. Marie Eckstein, the company's Global
Industry Executive Director, noted:

▶

*The revelation was that some people didn't care about that. The value proposition didn't work any longer. We were losing share to our competition, because we were trying to provide value at a cost that the customer did not want. Some of them wanted product on time with no service. 'Give us the lowest prices you got.' So that was a big revelation.*[2]

As a result of the research, Dow Corning completely rethought how it segmented its business. Instead of being organized by end-user applications or industries, it focused on needs-based segments with different requirements. These included innovative solutions (for the high end), proven solutions, cost-effective solutions, and price seekers (for the low end). The last group was the toughest one to address. It was growing fast and Dow Corning kept losing market share. Price seekers had little interest in what the company had always stood for – innovation, customer service and technical expertise in high-end solutions.

To compete in this segment, Dow Corning had to do something dramatically different. In 2002, the company launched Xiameter,[3] an online discount sales channel to keep cost-conscious customers and bring in new business. Through the website, customers could order products in bulk, at the lowest prices available, with little or no interaction with the Dow Corning salesforce. The targeted customers were those who knew two to four weeks in advance what their needs would be and how to handle their own technical services needs. Xiameter was clearly positioned as a separate sub-brand, distinct from the Dow Corning brand that was serving the segments with more demanding customer needs.

In parallel with Xiameter, Dow Corning introduced solution selling – aimed at customers who were willing to pay for total solutions and needed to interact closely with the company. Instead of the traditional approach of designing packages and then selling them, Dow Corning asked its customers what they were looking for and interviewed more than 500 members of its own salesforce.

In this segment, the company's sales culture went from being transactional to solution-based. The company developed and reinforced this new capability by means of training and by changing its incentive and reward systems. The initiative became part of Dow Corning's strategy of 'meeting customers' needs exactly.' For example, Dow Corning also offered consulting services to chemical companies looking to enter new geographic markets or improve the efficiency of their operational processes.

### Going for growth: Burns's 2004–2007 smart big move – rolling out Xiameter and solution selling

From 2004 onwards, new Chairman and CEO, Stephanie Burns, rolled out Xiameter and solutions selling. In 2005, the company posted $4 billion in sales, from more than 24 factories. Dow Corning had managed to reposition itself and, thus, remain the leader in silicone-based products, with a global market share close to 60 per cent. In the first three quarters of 2007, sales were $3.6 billion, up 13 per cent on the same period in 2006, and net profits were $523 million, up 20 per cent.

**Dow Corning's revenues and profits, 1995–2006 (million US$).**

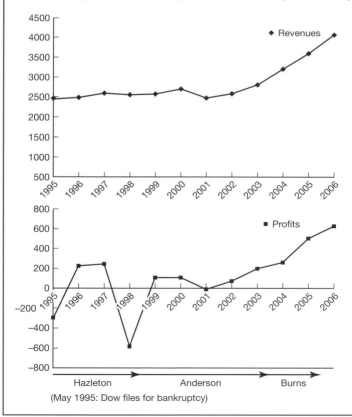

## Dow Corning's phases of development

**1950–1990** *Going for growth*, rolling out innovative products.

**1991–1995** Implant litigation forces Dow Corning into bankruptcy.

**1997–2000** *Failure to relaunch growth* – stupid big move of reorganization without distinctiveness.

**2000–2001** *Failure to relaunch growth* – stupid big move of trying to beat competitors at their own game with cost- and price-cutting.

**2001–2003** *Relaunching growth* – smart big move of repositioning with new segmentation and distinctive new brand for the low-end market, plus tailored propositions for other segments.

**2004–2007** *Going for growth* – smart big move of rolling out Xiameter and solutions selling.

# Distinctive Repositioning

Erik had agreed to read the case, as both Per and Caroline had crazy schedules for the next few days. With a trip to Switzerland planned, Erik knew that he would have the time to think about the notes that Bjorn was bound to have left with the case. Sitting in the lounge at Copenhagen Airport, Erik flipped to the notes:

*Why do executives think that they can reposition their companies profitably by copying the competition?*

- *Bandwagon effect* Drive to imitate increases when number of people doing it increases. Do I jump on the bandwagon or am I the only one stupid enough to lose out on the opportunity?

- *Imitation envy* Human tendency to mimic others with better performance driven by envy or social comparison that threatens our personal self-esteem – envy particularly intense when competitor perceived to be of similar or lower intrinsic capability.

- *Excessive optimism* Well over half the population believes they are above average on any particular activity they're engaged in. For example, managers regularly overestimate their ability to get synergies out of an acquisition or merger.

- *Illusion of control* Belief one can influence outcomes even when, in fact, one has no influence. This illusion predisposes leaders to greater risk-taking in trying to increase growth in the face of forces beyond their control.

- *External advisers* They may have an interest in an imitation move, such as investment bankers advising on potential acquisitions.

Erik could see how, at first, the Dow Corning people would have been dismissive of their new competitors' low-cost/low-price approach and, then, felt threatened as the new players ate into their market share. That was exactly how he felt about Oaty's new competitors. Psychologically, Dow Corning couldn't avoid the cost-cutting trend, just as he and Per had jumped on to the product diversification bandwagon. Also, because both Dow Corning and Oaty had been number one, they were sure they could win the competitive race, even possibly using pricing to control what happened to some of the weaker players.

Bjorn had, once again, picked the right case study. What was the solution, though? He was impatient for Bjorn to arrive. The two men had agreed to meet up at the airport before their respective flights left. Bjorn was off to the United States to go heliskiing.

At last, Bjorn strode into the lounge, taking a seat next to Erik. Erik barely greeted him before he asked:

'Bjorn, what's the alternative to trying to beat the competition at their own game? For Dow Corning, it was a question of segmenting the market into commodity versus service-sensitive customers. We've been trying different products for different customers and it hasn't worked.'

'The key is distinctiveness. To avoid making a big bet that backfires, avoid the "me too" bandwagon. For Dow Corning, new segmentation was only the starting point. The key to their repositioning was a radically different, no frills value proposition for the low-price segment. You've got to find what makes you distinctive. That's what'll give you a much surer move.'

'We've been looking at distinctiveness over the past weeks and months, but I'd appreciate your perspective. Any guidelines or pointers?'

Bjorn reflected before answering.

'One secret weapon is to look for things a growing segment of customers want but are not getting and to get rid of things they don't need but are paying for. Rather than "me too" imitation, take a contrary approach. In Dow Corning's case, the low-price segment was refusing to "overpay" for being "over served" and the solution was a website with a very limited range of products and no services, low and transparent pricing, an automated order fulfilment cycle and strict transaction rules.'

'That's not relevant in our industry.'

'Of course not. The point is to reposition with a new value proposition tailored to a growing segment that's not being properly served.'

Erik asked, intrigued.

'What might it be in our case?'

'If I knew the answer, I'd be one of your competitors.'

Bjorn pulled out his laptop.

'Let me show you another one of my favourite charts. This lists the different types of value proposition.'

**Relaunching growth: reposition the value proposition.**

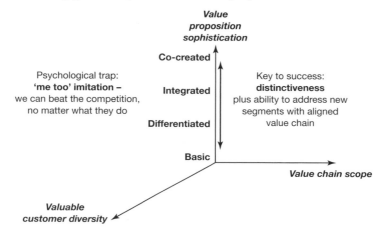

Erik looked carefully at the diagram.

'I presume that, for Dow Corning, their no-frills Xiameter brand would be an example of a "basic" value proposition, and then "differentiated propositions" was what they had been doing, and "integrated" was their new upmarket proposition of customer-specific innovation and services.'

Bjorn laughed.

'Hey, you're getting good at this conceptual stuff.'

'What in heaven's name is "co-created"?'

'Erik! You should know that from your previous life! It's when companies invite their customers to join them in creating new products, typically online. Most common are the media companies having consumers create content on their websites, but even players of the likes of Lego are inviting customers to design new Lego block applications on their website and selecting the ones with the most hits for commercialization. That's at the top of the diagram, though. It goes in increasing levels of complexity. First, you have the no-frills, "basic" type of value proposition, later you may try to differentiate yourself from your competition, then you integrate. The way to move on that axis is either to resegment your market and look for the white space or to come up with new products for existing segments.'

'Interesting, but I'm still at a loss to see how this helps Oaty.'

'The fundamental question is: what is it about Oaty that's distinctive from the competition? That's the best I can do for you, Erik. Gotta go – they're calling my flight.'

Erik looked at the copy of the diagram he'd made. What was it about the business that was distinctive, the basis for a new value proposition? He'd always felt that one of Oaty's distinctive features was the fact that it had no additives – it was a purely natural product. He remembered a one-pager that he had downloaded and placed in his bag with other reading material. The document was from the American Oats Society.[4] When he had found it on the Web, he felt that it might help with marketing Oaty. He looked at the page once more. Perhaps, it'd be more important than he thought.

## PROMOATING GOOD HEALTH

*The many benefits of Oats*

*Oat-based foods have long been known for their health benefits, and it's now general knowledge that oats make a significant contribution to human health.*

*According to the FDA, there is scientific agreement that soluble fiber from oat products when added to a low-saturated fat, low-cholesterol diet may help reduce the risk of heart disease.*

*In 1996, researchers at the Harvard School of Public Health found that in a study of more than 40,000 men, individuals with the highest levels of fiber consumption experienced a 35 percent reduction in the risk of heart attack compared to those with lower levels.*

*Oats are a great source of dietary fiber – they consist of approximately 55 percent soluble fiber and 45 percent insoluble fiber.*

*Tufts University researchers reported research results in the American Journal of Clinical Nutrition showing that eating a diet rich in oats significantly reduced both blood pressure and cholesterol.*

*Oats contain a high percentage of desirable complex carbohydrates, which have been linked to: reduced risk of colon, breast, and prostate cancer; better management of diabetes; and fewer bowel problems such as constipation.*

*Oats have a high Vitamin B1 content, which is required by the body for carbohydrate metabolism.*

*On a per gram basis, oats contain a higher concentration of protein, calcium, iron, magnesium, zinc, copper, manganese, thiamin, folacin and Vitamin E than any other unfortified whole grain, such as wheat, barley, corn or rice.*

*Oats contain one of the best amino acid profiles of all grains. Amino acids are essential proteins that help facilitate optimum functioning of the body.*

*Oats are naturally low in fat. Researchers agree that nearly everyone – men and women of all ages and races – benefits from eating a low-fat diet.*

*The lipids present in oats contain a good balance of essential fatty acids, which has been linked with longevity and general good health.*

**AMERICAN OATS**
OAT BASED PRODUCTS

As he came to the bottom of the page, it hit him! Of course, that was it – they needed Oaty to be recognized by the FDA![5] That would make the drink almost a 'functional food' and combine the best of both worlds: an organic drink for the lactose-intolerant that was also good for consumers' heart and cholesterol levels. That would make Oaty distinctive.

None of their competitors could make that claim – their primary target was natural food fanatics who were often active ecologists and vegetarians, but oats could provide people with much more than just these things, in the form of specific health benefits.

Now, what would shifting towards a functional food approach mean for how Oaty put together its value proposition? Maybe they should follow Dow Corning's approach and convene project teams – in Oaty's case, to develop oat-based diets for different types of people. The teams they had used in the past months, encouraged by Caroline, had been a lot more useful than he had expected, but could they stomach more projects after the painful re-engineering experience? What about exploring new distribution channels such as pharmacies and health clinics?

## Secrets of Relaunching Growth

The psychological trap is that we think we can beat the competition, no matter what they do.

To get to the top, we've had to compete, fight and win at many different points. This is one of the things that makes a business career exciting – the opportunity to measure oneself against others and see who's the best. The business success criteria are top- and bottom-line growth. There's no way we can accept falling behind in the growth race without a fight. After all, we're at least as capable as our competitors. The reference point is the best competitor in the game. If they're outpacing us, let's see what their secret is and adapt it for our purposes. Wait until we clean up our act and focus on the right things, then we'll see who's number one – we can beat them no matter what they do.

At Oaty, both Erik and Per were ready to take on their competitors in the product diversification game. Erik was ready because he had been first to go down that route with the loganberry flavour, but had to pull back when the market wasn't ready. Per was ready because his team was clearly the best in the industry at product innovation.

Dow Corning, coming out of bankruptcy, saw itself as the home of the best silicone technology worldwide. When some products became commodities, it decided to compete head-on by cutting prices. If that's what some competitors wanted to do, it'd show them who the leader was. However, no matter how determined it is, a premium product company cannot turn itself into a low-cost competitor without destroying at least part of its DNA.

## Smart Psychology

*For relaunching growth, the smart psychology is to get into the shoes of your top competitors (if necessary use your customers' views) and figure out how they would take additional market share and kill your company if you try imitation.*

At Oaty, Erik and Per had Bjorn and the case study to warn them about the dangers of trying to beat the competition at their own game with simple product diversification.

At Dow Corning, they first had to learn the hard way that cutting costs to compete with low-cost competitors wouldn't get them back into shape. Later, when Andersen took over, he asked the taskforces to get into the shoes of the customers to see how appealing the Dow Corning proposition was compared to the competition. They quickly found that 'the value proposition didn't work any longer' and there was no way Dow Corning could match the low-price competitors with its existing value chain.

## Smart Strategy

*The key to a smart strategy for relaunching growth is to find out what is truly distinctive about your company and leverage it into a distinctive value proposition – basic, differentiated, integrated or co-created– for a specific target market.*

Erik saw that oats are distinctive and that the company could use the specific health benefits of oats to turn Oaty into a FDA-approved functional healthfood.

At Dow Corning, the taskforces looked at what made the company distinctive: innovation, customer service and technical expertise. They figured out what types of customers valued this distinctiveness and what types didn't. This led to a new market segmentation based not on end-users but on customers' needs. Then they designed solutions with different levels of customization for the upper end of the market and the Web-based new brand, Xiameter – that is, a no-frills proposition for the low end of the market – a beautiful piece of smart, strategic thinking in a mature market.

## Smart Risk Management

*A common risk of imbalance in relaunching growth is that not enough attention is given to the link between distinctive product innovation and differing customers' needs.*

At Oaty, a functional healthfood would fail if they just put it out into the market and assumed customers would gravitate to it of their own accord. Success would require deeply understanding the diets and buying behaviour of customers with heart and cholesterol problems and tailoring a value proposition to their needs. Part of the secret of success of Xiameter was the precise tailoring of the new value proposition to the needs and wants of the low-end segment.

*The challenge of complementarity in relaunching growth is to design the new value proposition in such a way that it takes advantage of at least part of the existing value chain of activities.*

The more sophisticated types of value proposition – differentiated, integrated and co-created – all incorporate the basic proposition with added levels of functionality and perceived value. This means that they can share the basic operational capability. At Oaty, a heathcare proposition would add a dietary service, delivered through special channels, to the existing variety of oat milks – all manufactured in the same facilities.

At Dow Corning, all four value propositions were still silicone-based. Purchasing, technology and basic manufacturing were shared. The main difference in operations and distribution was between the bulk silicone sold through the online discount channel and smaller, specialized lots sold with increasing levels of service and customized innovation. The innovation, proven and cost-effective solutions could share manufacturing operations, but offered customers differing levels of sales, service and consulting expertise.

*The implementation risk in relaunching growth is that the taskforces don't think far enough outside the box to come up with a truly distinctive proposition and, if they do, the requisite capabilities are not developed to deliver it.*

At Oaty, Erik was thinking creatively enough to see the competitive advantage of a functional healthfood, but hadn't given any thought as to how Oaty would market and distribute it.

At Dow Corning, the taskforces comprised young turks – that is, the best middle managers and future leaders – who had the mandate to think way outside the box, which they did. For execution, the taskforces pointed out that the value chain would have to be reinvented. Dow Corning reorganized, setting up a separate division for the new Xiameter brand with a new, streamlined distribution channel at much lower cost, distinct from anything the low-cost competitors had yet tried. Special training and incentive and reward systems were developed for the sales engineers servicing the customer segments that wanted higher-value solutions.

The challenge in relaunching growth is to acquire or develop a new value proposition that is targeted and different enough to reignite growth while still taking advantage of at least part of the existing value chain of activities. This requires creative market segmentation, discovering what different types of customers value and don't value and then redesigning part of the value chain to deliver exactly what they want cost-effectively. All of this has to be achieved in a way that enhances the company's distinctiveness.

Restoring Profitability

"We always raise the stakes"

# 5

# Restoring Profitability

*Restoring profitability* is about focusing on the money-making parts of the business and restructuring by fixing, downsizing, divesting or closing the loss-making parts of the business. It's about refocusing the business model on the core elements of distinctiveness. Restoring profitability often becomes necessary after failing to get a business back into shape, as we saw in the case of HSBC when it failed to integrate Marine Midland and Household. It may be needed after taking a big bet that puts the business at risk, such as happened at Apple when it failed to relaunch growth with diversification or, as we shall see, when ABB failed to find a new game. It also may be the move required to save a business that is experiencing threats to its survival in the form of, for example, litigation and bankruptcy, as we saw at Dow Corning, or another external event, as in the case of Oaty.

**Restoring profitability.**

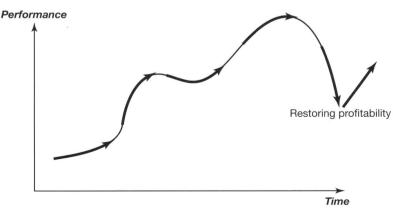

The common psychological trap in restoring profitability is that of trying to avoid the loss of face and pain involved in getting rid of the weak parts of the business and, instead, taking more risks by trying to relaunch growth or even finding a new game (see Beware Raising the Stakes next – believing that the way out is to move forward and be more daring). Success in restoring profitability comes not from taking more risk by trying something new but from taking less risk, simplifying and focusing on what already works, the money-making parts of the business (see ABB: Not More Risk but Bold Simplicity later in this chapter). To reduce the risk of failing to restore profitability, it is important not to take half-measures but to be realistic and bold in refocusing the business model (see Bold Restructuring near the end of this chapter). In the execution of restructuring, the need for a rapid response to avoid a crisis calls for a top-down approach, best done with a commander leadership style. The top management not only has to decide what to keep and cut but also has to implement with speed and a clear-cut process, later following up with taskforces to flesh out the longer-term vision.

# Beware Raising the Stakes

Marketing the benefits of oats in terms of lowering the risk of cholesterol problems and heart disease (in addition to helping those with lactose intolerance) proved to be a highly successful strategy. Oaty captured 38 per cent of the non-dairy drink market in Sweden and over 20 per cent in Germany and the United Kingdom. Even its launch in the USA was going extremely well, despite the competitiveness and maturity of the market – at least on the coasts – and the existence of established brands, such as Quaker.

Success hadn't come easily, however. After they had gained FDA recommendation, it took more time than anticipated to develop functional food research, marketing and a new distribution capability. It reminded Erik of the effort that had been needed previously to get the company's logistics in order. If he had a tendency towards excessive optimism, it was in estimating what it took to put a new organizational capability in place, but they'd done it and it felt good.

When the quarterly results came in, Per, Caroline and Erik celebrated at a new restaurant in Malmö. It was a true moment of détente, with the three partners discussing childhood memories. Erik thought back to his time at Software Inc. and congratulated himself on his decision to join Oaty. It was fun working with Per and Caroline, despite the occasional disagreement. It was also great to work with consumers rather than IT managers ... which is why they were completely unprepared for the call that came.

'Erik, get down here fast.'

Erik had never heard their purchasing manager sound so stressed.

'Where are you?'

'In Petter's field.'

When Erik arrived, followed by Per, he found a large group of farmers surrounding their purchasing manager. What was going on? Had he missed something? It was pouring with rain – why weren't they inside?

'Erik, look at the field.'

'What is this about?'

'Look at the field and tell me what you see.'

'Nothing. Just tall oats with red leaves.'

'Exactly.'

'What are you getting at? I'm getting soaked here.'

'Red leaves. BYD.'

'What?'

'Barley yellow dwarf virus. Its primary symptom is red leaves. It's everywhere.'

The news was terrible. The summer of 2007 had seen unusual weather, with temperatures reaching record lows and flooding in much of Denmark and southern Sweden. While oats is a crop that fares best in cool climates (growing as far north as Iceland), the heavy rainfall had ruined many acres. Erik was informed that BYD was a virus spread by aphids, the population of which was unnaturally high because of the unusually cool, moist weather. By the time the farmers observed and diagnosed the discolouration, it was too late. The symptoms are similar to those of nutritional disorder or nitrogen deficiency, making detection difficult. Because spring had come late, the cereals had been planted late, subjecting the crop to higher aphid populations and, thus, greater yield loss.

The destruction of a big part of the crop rippled through the entire business. Not only did it dramatically reduce Oaty's production capacity (most of the company's organic oats still came from Sweden) but Erik could also feel the farmers rapidly becoming more risk-averse. As much as he had come to appreciate the people from the farmers' cooperative, his business instinct was asserting itself. It told him that, to deal with this crisis, they would have to run alone in future – with a cooperative as a major shareholder, the decision-making process was too slow to manage a crisis.

During an action review meeting of major shareholders called two weeks later, Erik suddenly stood up. The animated discussions around the meeting room table stopped short.

Erik had stood up in sheer despair, the conversation was going nowhere and he had to think fast. Per was already looking at him with his 'be careful what you say now' eyes. Caroline nodded at him, encouraging caution. Erik took a deep breath.

> 'We have all been affected by the devastation to our crops. We have worked together to find substitute oats and keep the commitments to our main customers, but our cash flow is barely breaking even and will stay that way unless we take radical action. We will have to be bold.'

Sven, head of the farmers' cooperative, looked at Erik.

> 'Erik, what do you have in mind?'

> 'We need to rationalize the way that this company works. We have to make decisions faster, and we will have to restructure and downsize.'

> 'We can't do that!' Sven's reaction had been immediate.

> 'It's not whether we can or cannot – to survive, we'll *have* to. Companies restructure all the time. Jack Welch[1] said once that the only thing he regretted when he restructured GE was that he had

wanted too many people to be on board, that he could have moved faster, but had not been daring enough.'

'Erik, we don't need to restructure – we need a reliable oats supply and higher revenues.'

It was Per talking. He continued.

'We need to work more closely with our Polish subsidiary. We need to be innovative and expand our medical diet services into a fully fledged online advice platform. We need to tap into the high margins available in the healthcare business.'

Caroline stood up.

'Gentlemen, we have a reliable oats supply network here in Sweden. This red leaf problem will be over in a season. We can count on our Polish subsidiary for supplies. The challenge is not to lose our heads and make all kinds of radical moves. We need to keep cool and manage our way through this crisis, finding a solution that works for all of us.'

After elaborating on their positions, they were no closer to agreement. It was agreed that Erik, Per and Caroline would evaluate the options and come back in a week with an action plan. As the meeting broke up, Erik jotted down two bullet points:

- stop cash flow drain;
- redesign business model.

If there was one time he needed Bjorn's advice and case studies, it was now. Fortunately, Bjorn was his usual responsive self and, when he came over that evening, Erik quickly outlined the dilemma.

'The problems are greater than just the harvest. On the one hand, we need to stop the cash flow drain – we need to freeze all salary increases, halt expansion into new channels and markets and cut all product lines that aren't making money. On the other hand, we need to stop the revenue decline – we need to take advantage of this crisis to find alternative oat suppliers and redesign our business model to take advantage of the higher growth and margins in the healthcare business. Higher margins are essential if we are to absorb the increasing world market prices for cereals.'

Erik paused to take a breath.

'Per suggests – and I'm inclined to agree – that we expand our medical diet services into a fully fledged online advice platform. What do you say?'

'I read about red leaf in the paper and thought you might call. I'm not sure that taking on more risk with a completely new diet services platform is the right response to this crisis. Here's a case that I think you might find interesting.'

Erik stared at the name on the front of the case: ABB. *ABB*? Swedes didn't know whether to be proud of or embarrassed by the rise and fall and rise of the engineering giant. He was curious to find out how Asea Brown Boveri could help him with his own crisis.

## ABB: Not More Risk but Bold Simplicity

---

### ABB AB

*Relaunching growth: Percy Barnevik's 1988 smart big move – creating ABB by merging Asea and BBC, thereby repositioning them with a complementary product range and a highly decentralized organization to serve the fragmented market*

Agreed on in complete secrecy and announced to the world on 10 August 1987, ABB was created by the merger of the Swedish and Swiss electrical equipment firms Asea AB and Brown Boveri and Co. – the largest cross-border merger in European history. Overnight, the conglomerate became one of the world's leading producers of heavy electrical equipment. The company owned more than 700 entities, employed 160,000 people, had a presence in 25 countries and had $18 billion in annual revenues. Asea's CEO Percy Barnevik became CEO of the combined entity, as well as CFO and head of strategy.

Barnevik quickly appointed managers to run the business units serving the different product market segments and he called on these managers to think entrepreneurially, giving them a wide mandate for making decisions. Barnevik wanted a nimble organization

---

CHAPTER 5 RESTORING PROFITABILITY

with fast decision-making processes. In his opinion, success was 10 per cent strategy and 90 per cent execution.

At the same time, he dramatically reduced the corporate staff to just 140 people. ABB's loose matrix structure (geography and business), with English as the corporate language and a centralized financial control system (Abacus), kept the organization together. The merger and the tiny staff running such a large organization attracted media attention and everyone inside ABB felt special.

With the rising share price generated by the merger, Barnevik went shopping, acquiring more than 140 companies in the next 6 years and increasing its presence around the globe, including in India, China and the United States. ABB also ventured into businesses outside its traditional core, including engineering contracting, financial services and reinsurance. In the course of acquiring the Connecticut-based Combustion Engineering, ABB took on CE's liability for asbestos contamination – a development that many in the company would come to regret.

With the growth that came about because of these acquisitions, Barnevik had more and more difficulty running the increasingly spread-out ABB organization. He added a regional layer to the matrix, covering Europe, the Middle East and Africa, Asia and the United States. The regional representatives sat on the company's executive committee and only served to slow things down. The business units' managers didn't want to deal with the regional executive vice-presidents – they wanted to see Barnevik.

Yet, the company was widely perceived to be well managed, at the leading edge of technology and management thinking. In 1995, ABB was awarded Ernst & Young's Global Growth Award. The same year, Barnevik was awarded the European 'CEO of the Year' award.

***Getting back into shape: Göran Lindahl's 1996–1997 smart big move – responding to recession with geographic realignment of operations***

By 1996, the company had grown to 215,000 employees and $34 billion in revenues. The share value had increased fivefold and profits were healthy.[2]

▶

Barnevik stepped down as CEO, retaining the role of Chairman, and chose as his successor Göran Lindahl, a Swedish-educated engineer who was the group's Executive Vice-President in charge of power transmission and distribution. Lindahl also had geographic responsibility for the Indian subcontinent, Asia, the Middle East and North Africa, and had a reputation for bringing in large new contracts. Did Lindahl have the same kind of aura that surrounded Barnevik, though?

Lindahl chose not to pursue his predecessor's acquisition strategy. Unfortunately, this turned out to be a poorly timed decision. Revenues stagnated – a situation worsened by the recession in Europe, where ABB still generated 60 per cent of its income.

In response, Lindahl restructured the company, moving manufacturing to Asia, modernizing factories and firing 10,000 European employees. During the Asian crisis that followed, ABB benefited from low manufacturing costs, but the crisis also led to the cancellation of a $5 billion Malaysian project, which left ABB with uncovered costs of $102 million. In 1997 – when the *Financial Times* named ABB 'most respected company of the year' for the fourth consecutive time – the company's revenues dropped by 7 per cent, with net income falling by 54 per cent. Return on equity fell from 22 per cent in 1996 to 10 per cent in 1997.

**Failure to find a new game: Lindahl's 1998–1999 stupid big move – trying to reinvent ABB as a software services company without the necessary process capability**

Lindahl decided to completely redesign the company. He believed that ABB's international customers wanted a more global approach – that is, fewer visits from business unit salespeople and more people who truly understood their businesses. Lindahl shifted the balance of power from the country managers to business area heads. He reorganized ABB into seven business groups: power transmission; power distribution; automation; oil, gas and petrochemicals; building technologies; products and contracting; and financial services. Country managers no longer had responsibility for profits and losses.

Then Lindahl changed ABB's business portfolio. He wanted to reposition ABB as a knowledge and services company – the type investors favoured. He wanted to 'transform ABB from a traditional multinational industrial group into an agile, knowledge-based company dependent on intellectual assets rather than on heavy engineering assets. "Brain Power" was to be its corporate motto and the Internet its favourite tool.'

To get there, Lindahl divested the group's power-generation, railway equipment and nuclear power businesses. Disapproval was widespread. Many employees felt that, by getting out of the power-generation business, Lindahl had sold ABB's soul.

Lindahl then acquired software companies and two large power automation systems, Elsag Bailey and Alfa Laval Automation. At $2.2 billion, Elsag was ABB's biggest acquisition to date. Lindahl also ventured into alternative energy solutions. The change was radical: ABB went from being primarily a heavy equipment supplier to employing more software engineers than Microsoft.

In addition, Lindahl continued downsizing, closing 12 European factories and laying off more than 13,000 members of staff. Revenues increased by 6 per cent and net income by 180 per cent, while the share price doubled. At the end of 1999, *Industry Week* named Lindahl 'CEO of the Year' and ABB was listed on the New York Stock Exchange.

The dormant asbestos liability left over from ABB's acquisition of Combustion Engineering now suddenly turned into huge claims. These began to weigh heavily on the group's ability to deliver on an announced growth rate of 6 to 7 per cent by 2003. Lindahl decided to sell the company's share of the power-generation joint venture with Alstom for $1.2 billion.

Behind the scenes, disagreement grew between Barnevik and Lindahl. In October 2000, the two met to review the situation and it became clear that one of them had to go. It was Lindahl. He announced that he was stepping down as CEO, calling for someone with greater information technology skills to take the company to the next level.

***Failure to restore profitability: Centerman's 2000–2001 stupid big move – raising the stakes by moving to an even more sophisticated upstream–downstream business model***

Barnevik replaced Lindahl with Jörgen Centerman – a Swedish electrical engineer. Although a relative newcomer to the company's senior levels (he had joined the executive committee in 1998) he was credited with the smooth integration of Elsag Bailey.

Centerman immediately dismantled the corporate structure and executive team he had inherited. His vision was to pursue the shift to IT services, transforming the engineering, product-centric giant into a customer-centric, solutions-based company. Centerman reorganized ABB into 7 business divisions based on customer groups, with 4 serving end-users and 2 serving external partners, such as wholesalers and distributors. He set up 200 strategic accounts with key account managers caring for ABB's top clients – these representing 30 per cent of ABB's revenue.

There were two main hurdles to implementing the strategy. One was the conflict between country and business-area managers, which hindered the implementation of global standards and processes. The other was that ABB was not at all integrated globally – it did not even have a group website and functioned with more than 500 different ERP systems.

Centerman dealt with the first obstacle by doing away with country managers altogether – he saw the countries as a collection of business units that should report to a global business manager. This reduced the countries' responsibility, the sense of urgency and the local drive for results. In response, the business unit managers increased the number of 'key accounts' to protect their resources.

To tackle the lack of integration, Centerman took all of the functional processes away from the businesses, redesigning them as centrally owned shared services, then selling them back to the businesses. ABB's 'Group Process' taskforces spent 18 months trying to set transfer prices.

The company found itself floundering in the wake of the dotcom collapse. ABB had over $10 billion in debts due to acquisitions, asbestos claims, restructuring costs and share buyback issues.

During 2001, Centerman was twice forced to revise his revenue targets downwards. Even before the September 11 attacks on New York and Washington, DC, ABB's share price had dropped over 70 per cent. In November, Barnevik unexpectedly stepped down as Chairman amid a pension and payoff scandal. It appeared that both Barnevik and Lindahl had given themselves over $160 million in pensions and benefits without Board approval. The two later agreed to give back more than half.

Centerman announced that the company would cut its dividends and predicted flat revenues for 2002. At the year's end, ABB announced a loss of $700 million. In September 2002, Centerman was forced to resign.

### Restoring profitability: Dormann's 2002–2004 smart big move – refocusing the business model with bold simplicity

The new Chairman of the Board, Jürgen Dormann, stepped in to replace Centerman. The company's survival depended on how quickly he could turn things around. In his words, 'If ABB is around in 18 months, then ABB will be around for a long time.'

Dormann first simplified the organization, getting rid of unnecessary costs. Preoccupations with long-term strategy would come later. He sold off non-core businesses (such as financial services) and reduced the overall headcount to 100,000 people. With CFO Peter Voser, he negotiated a refinancing package and convinced shareholders to subscribe to new shares to reduce the company's debt. He killed the complicated Group Process initiative and re-established the power of the country managers. He disbanded the key account structure. He introduced a global scorecard for senior management and a stringent code of conduct, to prevent managers from being caught in opaque financial transactions when it came to multimillion-dollar global projects.

Eighteen months into Dormann's tenure, ABB had managed to resolve the nagging asbestos claims and divest all of its non-core businesses. The 'Step Change' strategy cut more than $1 billion from ABB's cost base. In 2004, earnings tripled compared with the previous year and two core divisions posted double-digit growth in both revenues and orders.

True to his statement that he would remain CEO for no more than two years, Dormann started looking for a successor. In February 2004, he announced that Fred Kindle – the CEO of Swiss technology company Sulzer – would succeed him, while he would stay on as Chairman.

**Going for growth: Kindle's 2005–2006 smart big move – facilitating roll-out to exploit the infrastructure boom**

ABB now had leading technology, a superb global distribution network and top talent out in the field that had stayed with the company. Kindle's task was to put ABB on a growth trajectory.

Kindle focused on execution as the key to ABB's future. ABB was failing to leverage its size to develop global purchasing power and economies of scale. Managers continued to reinvent the wheel. There were still more than 250 ERP suppliers. Global HR processes were lacking. Quality was wildly uneven. Also, cases of unethical behaviour from ABB's past kept popping up.

Kindle put in shared functional services, giving more decision making to global purchasing, improved financial control and compliance, made the company's HR services global and introduced large country and regional sales organizations.

His timing was good. The market for power and automation infrastructure started to take off, with rapidly rising demand – not only in the big, emerging market economies such as China and Russia, but also in the developed markets, which were struggling to refashion and upgrade their power grids. Between 2004 and 2006, ABB's revenues increased from $20 billion to $25 billion, with profits rising from $500 million to $1.5 billion. The share price rose from $5 to $18. In 2007, growth accelerated further so that, in the third quarter, revenues were up 26 per cent and profits 86 per cent compared to 2006, while the share price jumped to $30.

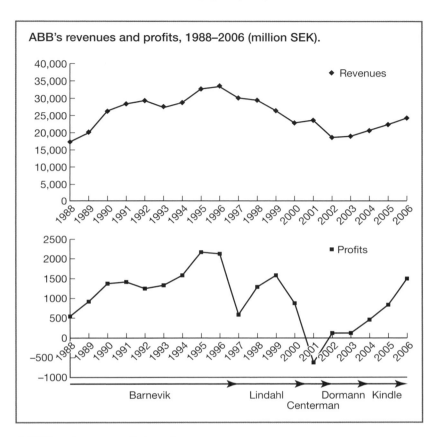

ABB's revenues and profits, 1988–2006 (million SEK).

## ABB's phases of development

**1988** *Relaunching growth – smart big move repositioning Asea and BBC as ABB.*

**1996–1997** *Getting back into shape – smart big move of responding to recession with geographic realignment of operations.*

**1998–1999** *Failure to find a new game – stupid big move of trying to reinvent ABB as a software company without the necessary supporting capability.*

**2000–2001** *Failure to restore profitability – raising the stakes by trying to reposition ABB with a more sophisticated business model without the supporting capability it needed to be effective.*

**2002–2004** *Restoring profitability* – smart big move of refocusing on the distinctive core of the company and restructuring.

**2005–2007** *Going for growth* – smart big move of rolling out core products to exploit the infrastructure boom.

## Bold Restructuring

The next morning, Erik walked over to Per's lab office. He got straight to the point.

'Per, what do you make of the ABB story?'

'Well, at least it's slightly closer to home than the HSBC one. Interesting that both ABB and HSBC grew through acquisitions and both ran into problems later. I also liked Percy Barnevik's fast-moving, decentralized organization – it created energy and entrepreneurship on the front line. As soon as they put in more organization to deal with the growth, things started going bad. I'm with him on that one – I've always hated bureaucracy.'

Erik sat down on the corner of Per's workbench.

'They didn't integrate their acquisitions. That created overlapping business units and they were each visiting the customers. Percy also took over Combustion Engineering's asbestos problem without doing his homework – that almost killed ABB. Bjorn would say that the acquisitions and growth knocked the business models out of balance and, instead of realigning their operations, ABB went for more growth.'

Per countered.

'I think Lindahl had bad luck. He tried to stop the acquisition game and ran into an economic downturn. He also tried to shift the balance from geographic organization and integrate with more emphasis on the business areas.'

'He wasn't very clever, though, when he tried to reinvent ABB with a big strategic shift from heavy assets to software without the company having any real experience in the area – and with no sense of whether or not that was what the market wanted. If ever there was a high-risk big bet, that was it. I wonder if it was his idea or Percy's? Maybe

Lindahl's biggest mistake was to take the CEO job while Percy was still Chairman of the Board.'

'Maybe, but my question is this: what does all of this mean for us? I still have difficulty linking these big-company stories to our situation.'

'Actually, with 144 million euros in revenues, we're not that small any more, but I'm with you. What's missing from this case are Bjorn's handwritten notes on the back. Those notes always make it clear why he thinks the case is relevant. Let's have him e-mail us those and see if he'll join us here after work.'

Bjorn's notes took only 20 minutes to arrive by e-mail.

**Raising the stakes**

• *Going for risk*: When faced with potential losses, people often become risk-seeking and raise the stakes, like in poker. Instead of restructuring, they go for a high-stakes new approach to the business. They want to reverse the negative situation, show that they haven't made a mistake, redeem their self-esteem.

• *Outcome bias*: They anticipate how good they'll feel when they succeed after raising the stakes. This positive potential dominates any serious consideration of the alternatives – especially the fact that they may fail with a more sophisticated approach.

• *Neglect of probability*: In the drive to try and correct the situation, they don't assess the probabilities of the possible outcomes. In particular, they underestimate the probable difficulties of developing new capabilities to support a new approach.

• *Pain avoidance*: Restructuring typically involves the emotional pain of parting with people, especially close associates. Raising the stakes is much easier emotionally.

## Smart restructuring

- Stop the cash flow drain immediately.
- Get rid of all loss-making activities.
- Refocus on the core elements of distinctiveness – the money-making parts of the business.
- Radically simplify organization and processes; get rid of costly complexity.
- Don't cut costs blindly – do it in a way that supports the refocused business model.
- Move fast; deal with resistance quickly.
- Avoid losing key people – remove their personal uncertainty by telling them quickly how they fit in.
- Give people light at the end of the tunnel by concentrating on the potential of the refocused business model.

When the three met later that day, Per and Erik were defensive.

'Bjorn, your notes are rather harsh. While I do think we need to change some things, your action points are quite drastic. I just think that the farmers are slow to move.'

Per chipped in.

'And I still think that what we really need to do is invest!'

Bjorn stepped in.

'I think your problems go further than red leaf and trying to speed up the decision-making process. Avoiding restructuring by going for a big bet and a more sophisticated model can be risky. Just look at Lindahl and, especially, Centerman at ABB. If ever there was a situation crying out for bold restructuring, it was ABB in 2000. The dotcom boom had crashed, asbestos lawsuits were threatening, and Centerman took the risk of introducing a sophisticated, customer-centric solutions and network-efficiency model. He should have done what Dormann did – use bold simplicity to reduce the risk and get back to basics.'

Bjorn drew the now-familiar three axes of the business model, this time with arrows pointing to the origin.

**Restoring profitability: refocus the business model.**

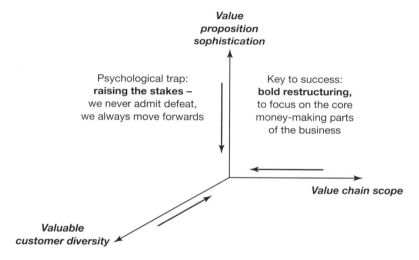

'The arrows show that restructuring is about going back to your core. You refocus and divest. For example, Dormann put in a committee of Board and management members to refocus ABB's strategy. Of course, refocusing or divesting calls for a strong top-down approach, with task-forces to make it happen. You've got to accept that it will be painful.'

Per remained sceptical.

'I presume what you're advocating for us is what Dormann did at ABB and what Erik wants to do here at Oaty – your so-called bold, simple restructuring. Well, I don't think it'll work here. I can't see our farmer cooperative shareholders ever accepting that.'

'Per, we've got to persuade them. The alternative is an accelerating slide into negative cash flow.'

'Erik, I refuse to argue with you about this again. Why don't you do the proposal for our shareholder meeting next week? I won't contradict you, but I'm not yet fully convinced. Let's ask Caroline what she thinks when she comes back.'

☆ ☆ ☆

Erik realized that this would be one of the most critical meetings of his business career. He put together a restructuring proposal similar to the one that he had talked about earlier, but he omitted Per's suggestion of trying to boost revenues by offering medical diet services. He included as much advisory support as possible to help the farmers to adapt.

The start of the meeting was difficult, but at least Sven agreed to let Erik explain the situation to the farmers. Then, they put Erik's proposal – to divest, close several subsidiaries and refocus their operations – to a vote. Erik had no more success with the farmers than he had had with Per. The cooperative voted down his proposal.

Per went underground and, apart from day-to-day issues, refused to talk to him about the future. The oats supply remained very tight and some key customers could not be supplied in a timely way so cancelled their contracts. Oaty had to cut costs fast to scale down with the declining revenues. Caroline was unable to reconcile the two men.

Erik decided that, to restructure properly, the company first had to buy out the farmers' cooperative. He approached an investment banking contact. He was surprised at how quickly they found a private equity firm that was seriously interested in doing a deal. However, his mood quickly soured when he learned how much debt the firm wanted to load on to Oaty to finance the cooperative buyout. When the private equity partners insisted that he increase his equity stake in Oaty and, if necessary, take out personal debt to do it, he exploded: 'Who do you think I am – one of the pawns in your Ponzi scheme?'

As he tossed and turned in bed that night, Viveka turned on the light.

'Why don't you drop Oaty and do something completely different?'

'Like what?'

'I don't know. Let's get some sleep – I have an important meeting to run tomorrow.'

☆ ☆ ☆

In the weeks that followed, the negotiations with the private equity firm proceeded far more rapidly than Erik had imagined – they seemed to really understand Oaty's business. All the issues were settled, except for Erik's role in the new organization. After an inconclusive afternoon round of negotiations, Erik reviewed the situation with Viveka.

'These guys want to box me in. To make this work, I have to be in charge, not hamstrung by all kinds of key performance indicators and debt covenants.'

'Erik, I have to say, this reminds me of what happened when you sold your software company. Seems to me, if you accept their terms, you'll land up being a glorified employee once again. Why don't you call a spade a spade and move on?'

'I can't just leave! Who's going to lead Oaty?'

'What about Per?'

'He's happiest leading the research team. He told me he doesn't want to worry about day-to-day stuff.'

'What about Caroline?'

'She doesn't have the experience.'

'What do you mean? She's got years of consulting experience. Didn't she get you guys to fix your logistics? Isn't she your COO? Don't tell me you're secretly biased against a woman taking the top spot?!'

'OK, OK, you may have a point.'

## Secrets of Restoring Profitability

The psychological trap is that we think we can never admit defeat, we must always move forward.

We didn't get to the top by buckling under at the first sign of real adversity. Rather, when more timid souls pulled back, we forged ahead. The ability to succeed against the odds is what turns us on and, as long as there is a chance of making it work, we go for it. The alternative, of saying we were wrong, is defeatist. Giving up on our business model and our colleagues is cowardly. They expect us to move things ahead. It's our role to take measured risks to grow our way out of the difficulty. That means being creative and courageous enough to develop a new approach to the business. We always move forward.

At Oaty, Per was not about to accept cutting back the business he'd put everything into developing. There was nothing fundamentally wrong with the business. It was a matter of riding out the rough patch caused by the oats disease. The farmers' cooperative was trapped in its role of supplier, not seeing its interests as a major owner. Even Erik, who saw the need to cut costs, believed that the company could grow the rest of the way out of the problem by developing an online diet advice platform.

At ABB, after the failure to find a new game in automation software solutions, Barnevik fired Lindahl and promoted Centerman. Instead of accepting the need to restore profitability, Centerman came up with a more sophisticated customer-centric business model with downstream customer-orientated divisions and upstream technology platforms. It was difficult for management at ABB – for so long admired as one of the world's best companies – to admit that it had made a fundamental error.

## Smart Psychology

*When there's a need to restore profitability, the smart psychology is to ask how you will explain to the markets and the Board why you bet the whole company on an unproven growth move rather than protect shareholder wealth by restructuring.*

At Oaty, Erik saw the need for restructuring more clearly after reading the case study. However, the dual role of the farmers' cooperative as supplier and owner blocked any psychological breakthrough for the others.

At ABB, Jürgen Dormann was first a Board member and then Chairman of the Board as the company's performance crisis deepened. (He had previously restored the profitability of the German pharmaceutical company, Hoechst, before managing its merger with Rhone-Poulenc.) He was fully exposed to the concern of ABB's shareholders and the financial markets and had to ask Centerman to leave. Those who don't see the need for profitability or who fail to restore it invariably have to go. Keeping this in mind is perhaps the best antidote to a misplaced raising of the stakes.

## Smart Strategy

*The key to a smart restructuring strategy is business model simplicity based on what is making or can make real money (returns above the cost of capital) and fixing, selling or closing loss-making activities.*

At Oaty, Erik was proposing to keep the confidence of the big, highly profitable clients by downsizing the rest of the business to fit the available supply of oats.

At ABB, Dormann got rid of all the organizational complexity and reorganized the company around its two core distinctive technologies – power and automation engineering. That meant unwinding the upstream–downstream divisions, killing the 'Group Processes' initiative, disbanding the key account structure and selling off the non-core businesses, such as financial services and building technology. It meant creating two simply organized functional divisions, power and automation, with the sales function controlled by the country managers. The 'Step Change' cost-reduction plan was put in place to reduce the cost base and consolidate the returns at a higher level.

## Smart Risk Management

*The biggest risk of imbalance in restoring profitability is indiscriminate cost-cutting that destroys the core distinctiveness of the business model.*

To preserve and capitalize on what is distinctive, investments may have to be made in the stronger parts of the business, while the weaker parts are cut back.

At Oaty, indiscriminate cost-cutting would have been a risk if they had tried to cut back across the board rather than distinguishing between the more profitable larger accounts and the less profitable smaller ones.

At ABB, when Lindahl cut costs and reorganized operations by moving manufacturing to Asia, he did not also question the newer software solutions businesses that were losing money and having difficulty acquiring profitable customers. Centerman's customer-centric model was way off balance on the operations side, especially when the 'Global Processes' initiative became bogged down. By contrast, Dormann achieved better balance by simplifying and giving sales and control to the country managers while bringing the factories back into the two product divisions.

*The complementarity opportunity in restoring profitability is to shed all activity that does not take advantage of distinctive capabilities or positioning.*

In the 1990s, ABB was unable to develop the integrated processes required to support software solutions, so it was an easy call to shed the latter during the turnaround in addition to the non-core activities. The difficulty lies with capabilities that are complementary, but not functioning properly. In ABB's case, both key account management and shared functional services are needed to make the global business model work effectively. They were discontinued during the turnaround, but later were reintroduced to support going for growth.

*The implementation risk in restoring profitability is either that management is not tough enough to drive through the change or that the restructuring drives away the best talent and destroys the future viability of the business.*

At Oaty, first, management couldn't gain agreement on the restructuring. Then, when it turned to a private equity firm to buy out the cooperative, the proposed incentive system made Erik question his own motivation.

At ABB, the big moves attempted by Lindahl, trying to find a new game, and, thereafter, Centerman, trying to relaunch growth, both faced so much resistance that they could not have succeeded without very strong leadership. Neither Lindahl nor Centerman were strong enough personally and, with Barnevik still present as Chairman, they didn't have the organizational authority to drive the change through. By the time Dormann took over as CEO and Chairman, the organization was looking for someone to save it. Dormann had both a quiet commander personality and the authority to make the turnaround happen. To motivate the frontline talent, he didn't try to do it all himself, but created the context in which the divisional presidents and their line managers could execute.

The challenge in restoring profitability is to start sooner rather than later, not think that you can avoid the pain by hanging on or forging even further ahead. It's essential to get rid of the obstacles and resistance to change as soon as possible with bold restructuring. The key objective is to protect and increase the cash flow by refocusing the business on the core, distinctive, money-making parts and consolidate that core as the foundation for future growth.

Secrets of Smart Big Moves

OAT MILK

The New York — Strong demand for oat milk!

FINANCIAL T — Best Brand of the Year: Oaty

© Doriane communication SA

# 6

# Secrets of Smart Big Moves

Erik looked up at the crowded auditorium and a brief moment of anguish seized him. Why had he accepted a faculty position at an elite business school? Common sense would have told him to just take it easy for a while. After he sold out his stake to the private equity firm, it was Per who'd jokingly pointed out an ad for an experienced case teacher. One thing led to another. He smiled when he thought back to his conversation with Bjorn.

'Remember those MBA discussions we used to have?'

'Sure, but now you'd probably have to do an EMBA given your age!'

'Actually, I'm going to teach them.'

'You're *what*?'

'Yes, well, I've accepted a posting in the United States, on the East Coast, as a professor of management practice. So, if you have any more good case studies up your sleeve, I'd be happy to see them.'

'What are you going to teach?'

'Smart big moves.'

'What, may I ask, is a smart big move?'

Erik's new students would have the same question. What he explained to Bjorn was now the basis for his teaching sessions.

'A *big move* is a shift in strategy involving a major commitment of resources. A *smart big move* is one that has a significant chance of creating great economic value – in other words, a strategic breakthrough. Reflecting on my experience, I see the five types of smart big moves depicted in the following chart.

**Types of smart big moves.**

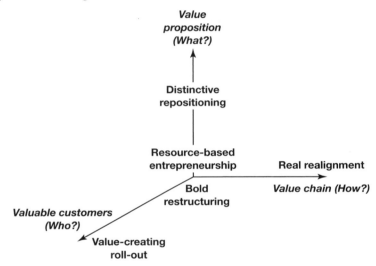

- **Experience-based entrepreneurship** is about *finding a new game* by capitalizing on an existing venture or leveraging an existing capability to create a breakthrough innovation or come up with an entirely new business model – what the company offers (the value propositions), who it is serving (new customer segments or markets) and how it delivers the value propositions to the valuable customers (the value chain of activities). Examples are Wipro's moves into hardware distribution, software services and then international information services, leveraging the earlier development of its hardware and software business, plus a network of overseas Indian contacts.

- **Bold restructuring** is about *restoring profitability* by simplifying and refocusing the business model on the core money-making parts of the business and fixing, selling or closing loss-making activities. Here, the classic example is the turnaround of ABB by simplifying the organization and refocusing the company on its power and automation businesses.

- **Value-creating roll-out** is about *going for growth* by taking a successful business model that creates value for customers and getting greater market share, extending it to adjacent customer segments and/or new geographies. Apple's roll-outs of the Mac, iMac, iTunes and iPod are examples of the resource focus that's needed to get even the greatest of products to live up to their full potential.

- **Real realignment** is about *getting* the company *back into shape* by ensuring that the value chain of activities really supports the value propositions and valuable customers by developing additional volume, process and/or network efficiency capabilities. HSBC's periodic initiatives to further integrate its financial services value chain with customer-orientated business divisions, then the 'Managing for Value' strategy and, later, 'Seven Pillars' of the organization, are relevant examples.

- **Distinctive repositioning** is about *relaunching growth* by developing new and distinctive value propositions of the basic, differentiated, integrated or co-created types for customer segments that may be new for the company but are already served by competitors. Dow Corning's development of the Xiameter value proposition for the low-end and increasing value for the upper-end segments is a classic example.

Even if most of the action is located on one of the dimensions of the business model – as in roll-out, realignment and repositioning – a big move invariably requires some change on the other dimensions as well.

It's also important to note that big moves can play out in many different sequences, depending on what is driving the strategic shifts. For example, when Oaty started up, the first move was about entrepreneurship, finding a new game. Then came going for growth with the roll-out of the basic oat milk product through the chain stores. After the premature attempt to diversify with a loganberry flavour and difficulties serving the large retailers, the next big move was getting back into shape through realignment of the value chain by means of improved logistics. As the competition caught up and the flavours proliferated, growth stagnated. Oaty had to look for a way to relaunch growth by repositioning its value proposition – marketing FDA-approved health benefits through new outlets. Finally, when the barley yellow dwarf virus hit, Oaty was forced to restructure its ownership in order to get shareholder support for downsizing to restore profitability.

Looking at these and other examples of the five types of big moves, both successful and unsuccessful, we can say that, to avoid a big bet and increase the chances of making a smart big move, a strategic shift must have three aspects:

- smart strategy
- smart psychology
- smart risk management.

If I had been aware of and followed through on these aspects during my business career, I would have avoided a lot of unnecessary problems. These three aspects contain the secrets of smart big moves, which I'm going to elaborate on in my classes.'

# Smart Strategy
## Think Smart Before Acting Big

The first thing that distinguishes a smart big move from a stupid one is that it's based on a smart strategy. It's a question of thinking through strategic shifts in a smart way *before* acting and, especially, before implementing a big move. Based on the management literature, there are relatively few features in a smart strategy that create economic value. They are:

- **distinctive capabilities** such as particular skills, process and culture, and/or positioning, such as access to resources, locations, technology or customers, relative to competitors
- **sustainable distinctiveness** that cannot easily be copied or will not soon disappear
- **attractive opportunities for growth** in the customer segments targeted by the value propositions.

The ways in which these characteristics of a smart strategy play out vary from one type of big move to another.

## Finding a new game

With the high risk associated with entrepreneurship, making the stretch to start a new game only makes sense when a new business model can be developed that is truly distinctive with large growth potential. The ability to deliver on the promise has to be checked out dispassionately.

In Wipro's case, each of its breakthrough business models was based on known technology augmented by existing or complementary services and cost advantages to create a distinctive first mover, addressing a large latent demand in the vacated Indian market before anyone else, then opening up the huge international market for outsourced information services.

## Going for growth

The value proposition is already making money and has proved its distinctiveness. To justify the dedication of large resources to the roll-out, the ability to create value for customers in the new markets must be there and the growth opportunity must be worth the effort.

Apple was successful with its roll-out of products to markets that were open and ready to pay for them, but unsuccessful when it tried to enter crowded markets where its design and software did not create additional customer value.

## Relaunching growth

The secret is to go back and evaluate what is truly distinctive about the company, then use that as a basis for a new value proposition – basic, integrated, differentiated or co-created – that is tailored to a specific target market. The new value proposition must be clearly positioned relative to the competition.

Dow Corning used its superior silicone technology as the basis for value propositions integrated with differing levels of its superior service for the upper end of the market and, at the lower end, exploited the Web to create a new basic, user-friendly, low-price, value proposition.

### Getting back into shape

The focus must be on getting costs under control with increased efficiency through better volume production, better processes or better network coordination. The objective is to gain a competitive edge by lowering costs in the value chain of activities and by enhancing the value proposition through the way in which it is produced and delivered.

HSBC increased efficiency first by focusing processes on customer divisions, then by putting in volume transaction processing offshore and, more recently, by coordinating its divisional and geographic network for cross-selling.

### Restoring profitability

The key to a smart restructuring strategy is bold simplicity, returning to the tried and tested elements of the company's distinctiveness that provide a basis for returns above the cost of capital.

ABB went back to the products based on the technologies in which it is a world leader – namely, power and automation – and back to distributing these through its global geographic network.

### Not smart strategy

Since these characteristics of a successful strategic shift are widely known, why don't we always make sure they're satisfied, especially when making a big move? It is because the irrational part of our brain often dominates the rational part, owing to the emotions and excitement associated with a big move. As a result, when making a big move, we frequently fall into psychological traps.

# Smart Psychology
## Don't Let Your Ego Trap You

When you make a big move, you're someone who is successful (otherwise you wouldn't have access to the resources) and ambitious. Successful, ambitious people achieve positions in which they encounter many temptations and enjoy the power to indulge their urges. They can construct masterful rationalizations to persuade others – and themselves – that what they're doing is right. They are clever enough to talk others into acceding to their wishes, even when what they are saying is disconnected from reality. Indeed, research shows that successful, ambitious people have higher opinions of themselves than do other observers of them. All of this makes them prone to hubris – that is, underestimating the challenges and overestimating their abilities.

Hubris shows up in many different ways. When it comes to big moves, it makes you underestimate the importance of the requirements for a successful strategy. For each of the big moves, one of the smart strategic requirements tends to be especially important and a related hubris often gets in the way of rational decision-making. Here's how different forms of hubris often come into play.

## Entrepreneurship

This is about finding a new game, of making new rules, coming up with an entirely new business model.

All the latest business research points to the importance of experience and/or a positional edge for both individuals and companies. Without experience, it is difficult to achieve sustainability. Yet, hubris makes successful managers think that they can run any business – all they need to find is a great opportunity. They fall into the trap of *opportunistic hubris* – *we can seize any opportunity, run any business.*

After the success with its hardware venture, Wipro's management believed that it could move just as easily into software.

## Roll-out

As roll-out involves a business model that already works, the key requirement is that of finding attractive opportunities – market segments with growth potential that want the value propositions you're offering.

The rational approach is to ask the market itself. Hubris, however, makes managers overestimate their understanding of the market and believe that they know what the market wants. They project their beliefs on to

the market and fall into the psychological trap of *inside-out projection –
we're the experts, we know what customers need.*

After succeeding with the Apple II, Jobs believed that the market would
accept the Mac and develop the software for it. Sculley and then Spindler,
after succeeding with the Mac roll-out, believed that the retail market
would want Apple-style consumer electronics and the business market
Apple-style minicomputers.

## Repositioning

This involves redesigning the value proposition to relaunch growth,
which means making it the most attractive proposition for a fast-growing segment.

The key requirement is distinctiveness relative to the competition.
Hubris makes managers believe that they can enter a fast-growing segment simply by beating the competition at their own game, rather than
doing the hard work of designing a proposition that is truly different
from the competition and tailored to an attractive market segment. As a
result, they fall into the psychological trap of *'me too' imitation – we can
beat the competition, no matter what they do.*

Coming out of bankruptcy, Dow Corning believed that it could beat its
low-cost competitors at the commodity product, cost-cutting game.

## Realignment

This is about ensuring that the value chain of activities fits the value
proposition and valuable customers, so the key strategic requirement is
alignment.

A rational manager would use the logic of consistency to see what needs
to be fixed, what new capabilities might need to be developed. Hubris
makes successful managers believe that they're doing better than they
are, denying anything is wrong. (The decline in performance is not
severe enough to make it undeniable.) As a result, they fall into the psychological trap of *narcissistic denial – we're the best, there's nothing wrong
with the business.*

After acquiring Marine Midland, CCF and then Household, HSBC accepted the views of the managements of those aquisitions that, despite the problems that led to their takeover, there was nothing wrong with their businesses.

## Restructuring

Restoring profitability requires the refocusing of the business model on the core elements of distinctiveness.

This means admitting defeat when necessary – letting go of businesses that aren't profitable and people who don't fit into the refocused business. No one likes admitting mistakes, however, and letting go involves psychological and emotional pain. Hubris makes managers think that they can avoid that pain by taking the risk of pushing for more revenues. As a result, they fall into the trap of *raising the stakes – we never admit defeat, we always move forward.*

At ABB, instead of restructuring, Centerman, with Barnevik still Chairman, raised the stakes and went for a more sophisticated business model based on customer centricity downstream and shared technology platforms upstream.

## Guidelines for mastering hubris

### Be open to facts that don't fit your preconceptions

- Don't rationalize away uncomfortable data.
- Integrate it into your thinking.
- Ensure that the facts are consistent with value-creation.
- If not, the big challenge is that you may have to abandon your pet project.

To gain access to these less obvious facts, you must create additional 'personal bandwidth' – that is, mental space to see, hear and understand what's really going on, especially the undercurrents and deeper trends. To do this:

- open up time in your agenda;
- put new activities on the agenda;

- avoid the seductive charm of having people tell you what they think you want to hear – expose yourself to different types of people, especially those willing to question.

### Accept wide-open dialogue

- Use your boss, mentors and Board members as checks and balances – even as sparring partners.
- Pay attention to appropriate organizational processes – don't short-circuit them in pursuit of big moves.
- When was the last time you and your team put the brutal facts on the table?

### Avoid being influenced

- By paid service providers, such as investment bankers, consultants, accountants – they are more interested in being paid than giving you impartial advice.
- By professional peer groups who are in friendly competition with you and, therefore, have a subconscious interest in coming out ahead.

### The critical people to expose yourself to varies with the type of big move

- *For entrepreneurship, venture capital*-type opinion can be useful, to ensure that you have a compelling new business model and you don't assume managerial expertise trumps industry-specific capabilities.
- *For roll-out,* the *customers'* views are essential to ensure that you create value for them. Put yourself in the shoes of your new customers to see what your value proposition looks like from their point of view.
- *For repositioning,* the *competitors' perspective* is essential, to ensure that you don't try to beat them at their own game. Step into the shoes of your top competitors to see how they will respond to your new value proposition.
- *For realignment, frontline employees'* opinions are essential because they know what needs to be fixed and their commitment will be necessary to make it happen. See whether or not their critique reflects where the business is on its trajectory.

- *For restructuring, financial analysts'* opinions can be useful because their valuations depend on understanding the core elements of distinctiveness. To avoid raising the stakes, ask whether or not you could defend betting the whole company on an unproven growth move.

### Work from the outside in

- Get feedback from the opinion leaders mentioned above and expand your circle of regular contacts to include them where necessary.
- Put yourself in their shoes.
- Be proactive and test their reactions to proposed big moves face to face.

### Learn from past mistakes

- Awareness of past experiences is probably the best antidote to falling into the traps of hubris. When he came back to Apple, Steve Jobs had been chastened by his experience outside and was much more realistic, not trying to create new markets, but addressing those that already existed. Azim Premji at Wipro also learnt the hard way that a software capability had to be developed incrementally. At ABB, by the time he took over, Jürgen Dormann knew from his experience at Hoechst and Aventis that turnarounds have to be built on bold restructuring.

- When we don't learn from past experience, we set ourselves up to repeat the mistakes of the past. At Dow Corning, it took five years of declining results before management realized that it had to do something distinctive. At HSBC, as in the rest of the banking industry, each new generation of managers seems to have to relearn that you should not make acquisitions without integrating them and you can't lend money to people who can't pay it back.

## The secrets of smart psychology. In a nutshell:

Really listen to the right people, modify decisions when necessary and, above all, learn from experience. As historian Barbara W. Tuchman put it, after investigating stupid political moves:

*The overall responsibility of power is to govern as reasonably as possible ... A duty in that process is to keep well-informed, to heed information, to keep mind and judgment open and to resist the insidious spell of wooded-headedness. If the mind is open enough to perceive that a given policy is harming rather than serving self-interest, and self-confident enough to acknowledge it, and wise enough to reverse it, that is a summit [in the art of leadership].[1]*

# Smart Risk Management
## Avoid Jumping, Learn to Run

Smart risk management is about avoiding three frequent types of execution risk associated with big moves.

- *Unbalanced business model* The three dimensions of the what, who and how no longer fit together and create the subsequent need for another big move to rebalance the business model.

- *No complementarity between new and existing capabilities* This makes it impossible to leverage existing experience and increases the chances that the desired new capabilities will fail to take root in the organization.

- *Inappropriate implementation process and leadership style* This makes it virtually impossible to get the emotional commitment of employees needed to execute the big move.

Let's look at how we can mitigate these risks in order to execute strategic breakthroughs.

### Periodically rebalance the business model with a big move on a different dimension

The three dimensions of the business model have to fit and work together as suggested in the figure.

**How the three dimensions of the business model work together.**

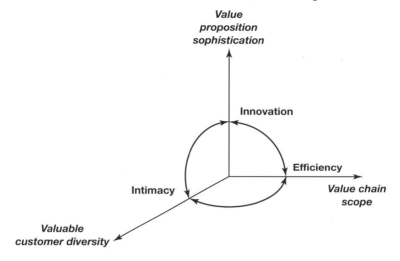

While each of the business model's dimensions must be at work at all times, it is difficult to pursue them with equal intensity. *Innovation* typically calls for a looser organization with room for experimentation, entrepreneurship and flexible resources. *Efficiency* depends on greater coordination, leveraging activities in the business system and removing slack from the organization. *Customer intimacy* requires a culture of listening and networking, with resources directed at building relationships with them.

Errors involving a lack of capability development – or excessive development of one dimension at the expense of the other two – destroy the balance in the business model. Examples include growing so fast that efficiency lags behind innovation and customer intimacy, cutting costs so much that innovation and customer intimacy become atrophied or paying so much attention to customers that fundamental innovation and costs suffer. As a result, when badly executed, each of the big moves can cause different types of imbalance in the business model.

- *During entrepreneurship* a common imbalance is the focus on product and value proposition development at the expense of customer acquisition and delivery.

- *During roll-out* the energy put into opening up new markets often is accompanied by a lack of attention to value chain capability and capacity.

- *During repositioning* the attention given to redesigning the value proposition often comes at the expense of attention to the link to differing customer needs and delivery capability.

- *During realignment* there may be an excessive focus on efficiency to the detriment of product innovation and customer intimacy.

- *During restructuring* the biggest risk of imbalance is indiscriminate cost-cutting that destroys the core distinctiveness of the business model.

Re-establishing the balance between innovation, efficiency and customer intimacy capabilities is a challenge. Companies often oscillate between the dimensions as the business evolves. A typical cycle might involve getting closer to customers to stimulate the top line by going for growth with a roll-out. Focus on the value chain might follow to improve margins by getting back into shape or, if necessary, restoring profitability. Then there might be an emphasis on innovation to reposition the value proposition and relaunch growth or entrepreneurship may be employed to find a new game.

In the histories of Wipro, HSBC and ABB, big moves that involved growth (finding a new game, going for growth or relaunching growth) were followed by either a move to get back into shape or a failure due to another attempt to grow the top line. Apple and Dow Corning succeeded with two or more successive moves to grow the top line, but only after almost a decade of failure followed by moves to restore profitability. In general, we can say that, after growing the top line, the next smart move is to really check the balance of the business model and, if necessary, get back into shape before making another big move to grow the top line.

## Leverage existing experience by developing complementary capabilities

Capabilities can build on and complement each other in many ways. One development sequence of complementary capabilities starts with finding a new game – the *pioneering innovation* and potentially disruptive applications that open up a new value proposition cycle.

Once the basic value proposition has been standardized, the stage is set for roll-out to a mass market based on *volume efficiency*. However, the emphasis on efficiency is at the expense of innovation. This opens up the potential to extend the roll-out with *differentiating innovation* to provide more variety in product features, design and marketing.

Controlling the costs created by increased variety typically calls for getting back into shape, with *process efficiency* obtained through the re-engineering of activities and continual improvement. Once again, the drive for efficiency often drowns out both innovation and the voice of customers.

Given the wide range of value propositions available at this stage, customers are often looking for some way of pulling it all together. This makes it possible to relaunch growth again, using *integrating innovation* to solve customers' problems and/or create a total experience by combining customers' understanding, consultation and the various value propositions to deliver a tailored solution.

Making it work calls for getting back into shape, with integration across internal and external organizational boundaries. Cost-effective integration requires *network efficiency*, optimizing the coordination of partners and activities in the value chain, with outsourcing, in-house expertise centres and production platforms.

When the network is extended to include customers, they can then be invited to relaunch growth by participating in the *co-creation* of new value propositions.

This particular sequence of complementary capability development is reflected in the diagram overleaf.

Complementary capability development.

There are many other possible sequences of complementary capability development. Some companies, such as Rolex, have mainly expanded the diversity of their valuable customers. Others, such as Toyota, have evolved mainly along the axis of increasing value chain efficiency. Whatever the learning logic, the development of a basic value proposition through pioneering innovation must precede the creation of incremental variety with differentiating innovation and this variety is the basis for integrating innovation. In terms of the value chain, a value proposition standard is required for volume efficiency, which is the platform needed for process efficiency, without which network efficiency is impossible.

The histories of Wipro, Apple, HSBC, Dow Corning and ABB show that trying to find a new game, going for growth or relaunching growth without the necessary supporting capabilities inevitably fails, no matter how talented the management or how successful the company has been so far. In addition, it is impossible to make an organization suddenly acquire and successfully exploit new capabilities that are not complementary and integrated with those already in place. See, for example, Wipro's first move into software, HSBC's move into statistical consumer finance or ABB's attempt to offer complex engineering solutions in the late 1990s.

Learning logics can be broken at any moment by someone finding a new game based on a new disruptive technology or the creation of a new product or market segment or by external events originating outside the industry. Wipro had to adapt to the sudden opening of the Indian market, Apple had to deal with the PC price wars, HSBC with the subprime crisis, Dow Corning with the implant litigation and ABB with the dotcom crash and asbestos litigation.

Because the internal learning logic is broken, the implementation of the big moves needed in these situations is especially challenging. Wipro exploited the external shock to its advantage because Premji had seen it coming. HSBC dealt expeditiously with the subprime crisis, because it had had two previous experiences with a collapsing mortgage market in the UK and Hong Kong. By contrast, the external shocks pushed Apple, Dow Corning and ABB into periods of severe losses before they turned things around and restored profitability. All three companies were fortunate to find experienced leaders (Jobs, Andersen and Dormann) to focus them and restore profitability.

## Use an implementation process and leadership style appropriate to the time available and resistance to the big move

Smart big moves typically are made up of a sequence of two or more change processes.[2] The key attributes that distinguish the different change processes are:

- speed – faster or slower;
- source of energy – more from the top or more from the whole organization.

The speed that is appropriate depends on the time available to shape or respond to the forces of change.

There are a number of situations in which speed is critical. In rapidly deteriorating or crisis situations that require restructuring, a fast response is essential if the business is to be saved. Rapidly closing windows of opportunity – such as first-mover advantages during entrepreneurship and roll-out – also call for fast reactions if the opportunities are not to be lost.

At the other end of the spectrum, during realignment and repositioning, slower changes may be called for to allow enough time to build new capabilities or change the organization's culture. Time is also needed to gauge the success of experimentation and pilot projects. Speeding up the process could jeopardize the whole initiative.

The appropriate source of organizational energy depends on whether change needs to be driven from the top down to overcome resistance or the entire organization has to be energized to drive the change. If people are not ready and/or willing or are going in the wrong direction – for example, prior to restructuring – the top must provide more energy to put the change on the right path. Energy from the top is also necessary when only a small group is involved in the change – for example, in re-engineering processes during realignment or, during repositioning, adding new product lines or making portfolio acquisitions for growth.

On the other hand, when people are ready, the whole organization can be mobilized. This is critical for changes in culture and behaviour, the development of new capabilities or large-scale programmatic changes during the later phases of repositioning and realignment. More energy from the whole organization is especially important for fast-moving, bottom-up initiatives to respond rapidly to customers' needs or bring innovative products to market and grow the top line during roll-out and entrepreneurship.

The figure below depicts four classic change processes in terms of their relative speeds and sources of energy, as well as change paths (sequences of processes) frequently associated with the different types of big moves. While all four processes are usually initiated at the top, they can differ significantly in terms of speed and source of change energy.

**Common change paths for big moves.**

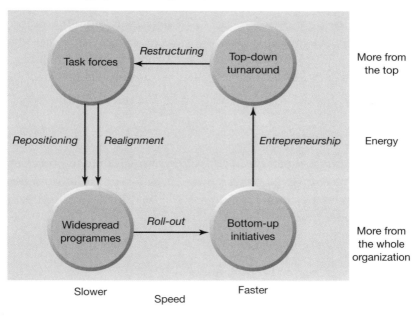

Entrepreneurship typically has its origins in a promising frontline initiative or venture around which the company is then reconfigured top-down. At Wipro, Premji brought in Sridhar Mitta first to reconfigure the business for hardware distribution, and then Vivek Paul to reconfigure it for international software services.

Roll-out often requires a widespread programme to get everyone properly trained and is then executed through bottom-up initiatives on the front line. At Apple, Jobs ensured that the necessary capabilities were in place and energized the front line for roll-out.

Realignment often starts with taskforce re-engineering of the value chain and repositioning with taskforce exploration of new value propositions before both moves are embedded in the organization with widespread programmes designed to provide the required supporting capabilities. HSBC regularly uses project taskforces to redesign the value chain before deploying the new processes with corporate-wide programmes. At Dow Corning, taskforces of future leaders redesigned the value propositions before they were embedded with extensive training programmes.

Restructuring typically starts with a top-down elimination of unprofitable activities, followed by taskforce determination of how the company should be refocused for long-term success. At ABB, Dormann and his CFO, Peter Voser, did the initial restructuring before a strategy taskforce was put together to chart the future course of the company.

Smart big moves can only succeed if each change process in a path is properly executed. Below are some of the essential success factors for each of the four processes.

- *Top-down turnaround (fast, energy from the top)* Precise, objective, detailed plan; early action against resisters; fast execution with frequent follow-up; transparent; walk the talk; long-term vision to prevent poor morale. Typical leadership style is that of a *commander*, *directing*, often using shock treatment to create a sense of urgency. Danger: if the direction is wrong, possible catastrophe; if buy-in is weak, slow change on the front line.

- *Taskforces (slow, energy from the top)* Steering committee; sell need for change to rest of organization; clear mandates for taskforces; resource with good people and real time; manage the portfolio of taskforces. Typical leadership style is that of a *chairman, orchestrating*, often using quick taskforce wins to build support. Danger: taskforce pollution, no closure, no roll-out.

- *Widespread programmes (slow, energy from whole organization)* Top-management workshop to set clear targets; cascade down organization with disciplined process; widespread involvement in programme process; seminars, conferences, events. Typical leadership style is that of an *organizational coach, facilitating,* often using brutal facts and scenario-building to achieve sense of urgency. Danger: slow, warm feelings, no results.

- *Bottom-up initiatives (fast, energy from whole organization)* Aspirational goal; multiple accesses to ideas, talent and resources; incentives and protection from failure; working framework and guidelines; concrete milestones; manage the portfolio. Typical leadership style is that of a *catalyst, inspirational,* often using exposure to customers, competitors, analysts, other outsiders to create urgency. Danger: confusion, chaos.

# Epilogue

Erik found his first year adapting to a new life as a professor of management practice quite hectic and, apart from some pleasantries exchanged over the phone, he lost touch with his former colleagues. On the plane on the way back to Sweden for the summer break, his mind drifted back to his experience at Oaty. How fortunate they had been to have such a well-balanced management team, before the private equity people came in!

He, Erik, had been the commander, with a preference for moving fast and making things happen. Per was the research catalyst who preferred to manage bottom-up by letting people do it themselves. Caroline was the organizational coach who knew how to put processes in place to develop capabilities. Finally, Bjorn, while not formally on the management team, played the role of the chairman leader, trying to get the team to look at the facts before jumping to conclusions.

Soon after he arrived, Erik went to see Per. He was especially curious to find out how he was managing the relationship with his private equity shareholders.

'How are you guys doing? I've heard that you've turned the business around and Caroline is doing very well as CEO.'

'With alternative oats suppliers in Poland and the United States, things have been picking up quite rapidly. We're almost back to our earlier levels of revenue and we're starting to look into expanding our medical diet services platform. As you predicted, it's much easier without the farmers as shareholders. Caroline has adapted her style to take over your role as well. You'd be surprised how directive she can be when the need arises.'

'What about your private equity partners? How are you getting on with them?'

'Rather well, actually. Bjorn's been a big help.'

'You mean he's still handing out more case studies?'

'No. Believe it or not, he's become one of the private equity partners.'

'What?'

'He's one of the most helpful of the Board's members.'

Erik considered the startling news.

'Of course – that's why he's been a little coy on the phone over the past year and why he was so forthcoming earlier with his cases. The big business guy secretly wanted to be an entrepreneur!'

'And the entrepreneur secretly wanted to be a business professor. That's why he was so interested in the cases and charts!'

'You're right, Per. You know what I've discovered over the last year? The business school professors secretly want to be big business guys. That's why they write the cases!'

## The End

# Endnotes

## Chapter 1

1 'Oatmeal in a Glass'. We can thank a group of Swedish farmers and scientists for inventing oat milk. Richard Oste, PhD, assistant professor of biochemistry at Lund University in Sweden, developed the process. Called the Oste Process, it uses oat kernels and rapeseed (canola) oil to produce a neutral-tasting, highly stable beverage that is also an excellent substitute for cow's milk in cooking and baking. Oat milk contains vitamin E and folic acid and is low in fat and contains amino acids, vitamins, trace elements, and minerals. The extraction process allows much of the natural fiber to remain in the final product, which makes oat milk "oatmeal in a glass". See www.swedish.org/16356.cfm

2 Martin N. Davidson, Gerry Yemen and Heather Wishik, *Wipro Technologies Europe*, Darden Case No. UVA-OB-0755, 2004.

3 Lynn Sharpe Paine, Carin-Isabel Knoop and Suma Raju, *Wipro Technologies*, Harvard Business Case 9-301-043, 2001.

4 Steve Hamm, *Bangalore Tiger: How Indian tech upstart Wipro is rewriting the rules of global competition*, McGraw-Hill, 2007.

5 Ibid., page 34.

6 Ibid., page 39.

7 The Software Engineering Institute at Carnegie Mellon University developed the certification for the US Department of Defense to measure the quality of its suppliers.

8 Hamm, *Bangalore Tiger*, page 21.

## Chapter 2

1 Jeffrey S. Young and William S. Simon, *iCon Steve Jobs: The greatest second act in the history of business*, John Wiley, 2005, page 93.

2 G. Pascal Zachary, 'Apple plans to launch product lines aimed at consumer electronics markets', *Wall Street Journal*, 10 January 1992, page B8.

3 'Apple tumbles to the ground', *The Economist*, 28 August 1993.

4 Lex column, *Financial Times*, May 1996.

5    Stewart Alsop, 'My old flame: the Macintosh', *Fortune*, 25 June 2001.

6    R. White and K. Mark, *iPod, iTunes and Fairplay*, Richard Ivey School of Business Case Study B06M080, 2006.

7    M. J. Epstein and J.-F. Manzoni, 'Reflections on the human implications of the search for performance', in M. J. Epstein and J.-F. Manzoni (eds), *Performance Measurement and Management Control: Improving organizations and society*, Elsevier Science/JAI Press, 2006.

8    Apple's Newton PDA introduced handwriting recognition software, but it was notoriously inaccurate – at least at first – and the device's high price kept sales far below expectations.

9    Although Amelio warned the Board that he would need at least 3 years to turn the company round, the Board abandoned him for Jobs after 18 months.

## Chapter 3

1    www.organicmonitor.com

2    P. Strebel and B. Rogers, *HSBC: Strategic Evolution of the World's Local Bank*, Case Study IMD 3-1586, 2005.

3    T. Khanna and D. Lane, *HSBC Holding*, Harvard Case Study 9-705-466, 2006.

4    www.hsbcamanah.com/1/2/investor-relations/strategy

5    Ibid.

## Chapter 4

1    http://ourworld.compuserve.com/homepages/stevecarper/uknews.htm

2    Charles Butler, 'Dow Corning's extreme makeover', *CRM Magazine*, June 2004; P. Werhane and J. Stocker, *Dow Corning Corporation (A)*, Case Study UVA-E-0104, 1997; P. Werhane, B. Cunningham and J. Stocker, *Dow Corning Corporation (B)*, Case Study UVA-E-0148, 1997; P. Werhane and B. Cunningham, *Dow Corning Corporation (C)*, Case Study UVA-E-0149, 1997.

3    K. Kashani, *Xiameter: The past and future of a disruptive innovation*, Case Study IMD-5-0702, 2006.

4    www.americanoats.com/benefits.html

5    The FDA approves drugs, but for natural products it may in some cases recognize specific health benefits without the products having to go through the lengthy process required for drugs.

## Chapter 5

1  Ex CEO of General Electric.

2  References for this information and that in following pages: P. Strebel and N. Govinder, *ABB Leadership (A–D) 1998–2002,* Case Study IMD-3-1241 to 1244; *ABB Governance (A–D) 2004,* Case Study IMD-3-1471 to 1474.

## Chapter 6

1  Barbara W. Tuchman, *The March of Folly: From Troy to Vietnam,* Knopf, 1984, page 32.

2  P. Strebel, *Sequencing Change in the Pursuit of Better Performance,* IMD Perspectives for Managers, 2006, pages 1–4; P. Strebel, *The Change Pact: Building commitment to ongoing change,* Financial Times Pitman Publishing, 1998.

# Bibliography

Chandler, A.D. (1962) *Strategy and structure: Chapters in the history of the industrial enterprise.* MIT Press, Cambridge, MA.

Dosi, G., Nelson R.R. and Winter S.G. (eds) (2000) *The nature and dynamics of organizational capabilities.* Oxford University Press, Oxford.

Epstein M. J. and Manzoni, J. F. (eds) (2006) 'Reflections on the human implications of the search for performance', in *Performance measurement and management control: Improving organizations and society,* Elsevier Science/JAI Press.

Gibbons, P.T. (1992) 'Impacts of organizational evolution on leadership roles and behaviors', *Human Relations,* 45(1): 1–18.

Hammer, M. and Champy, J. (2003) *Reengineering the corporation: A manifesto for business revolution.* Harper Business, New York.

Kets de Vries, M. (2001) *Struggling with the demon: Perspectives on individual and organizational irrationality.* International Universities Press, Madison, N.J.

Killing, P., Crossan, M.M. and Fry, J.M. (2002) *Strategic analysis and action.* Prentice Hall, Toronto.

Lawrence, P.R. and Lorsch, J.W. (1986) *Organization and environment.* Harvard Business School Press, Boston.

Miles R. and Snow C. (1978) *Organizational strategy, structure, and process.* McGraw-Hill, New York.

Miller, D. and Friesen, P.H. (1977) 'Strategy-making in context: ten empirical archetypes', *Journal of Management Studies,* 14: 253–279.

Miller, D. and Mintzberg, H. (1984) *Organizations: A quantum view.* Prentice Hall, Englewood Cliffs, N.J.

Quinn, R.E. (1988) *Beyond rational management: Mastering the paradoxes and competing demands of high performance.* Jossey-Bass, San Francisco, CA.

Read, S. and Sarasvathy, S. (2005) 'Knowing what to do and doing what you know: effectuation as a form of entrepreneurial expertise', *Journal of Private Equity*, 9(1): 45–62.

Romanelli, E. and Tushman, M. (1994) 'Organizational transformation as punctuated equilibrium: an empirical test', *The Academy of Management Journal*, 37(5): 1141–1166.

Roxburgh, C. (2003) 'Hidden flaws in strategy', *McKinsey Quarterly*, p. 27–39.

Strebel, P. (1988) 'Rebalancing the organization: key to outpacing the competition', *IMD Perspectives for Managers*, p. 3.

Strebel, P. (1989) 'Competitive turning points: how to recognize them', *European Management Journal*, 7(2): 141–147.

Strebel, P. (1992) *Breakpoints: How managers exploit radical business change*. Harvard Business School Press, Boston.

Strebel, P. (1994) 'Choosing the right change path', *California Management Review*, 36(2): 29–51.

Strebel, P. (1995) 'Creating industry breakpoints: changing the rules of the game', *Long Range Planning*, 28(2): 11–20.

Strebel, P. (1998) *The change pact: Building commitment to ongoing change*. Financial Times Pitman Publishing, London.

Strebel, P. (2003) *Trajectory management: Leading a business over time*. J. Wiley and Sons, Chichester.

Strebel, P. (2006) 'Sequencing change in the pursuit of better performance', *IMD Perspectives for Managers*, p. 1–4.

Strebel, P. and Ohlsson, A.V. (2006) 'The art of making smart big moves', *Sloan Management Review*, p. 79–83.

Tuchman, B. W. (1990) *The march of folly: From Troy to Vietnam*, Abacus, London.

Tuchman, M.L. and Romanelli, E. (1985) 'Organisation evolution: a metamorphosis modelof convergence and reorientation', in Cummins, L.L. and Staw, B.M. (eds) *Research in organizational behaviour*, pp. 171–222. JAI Press, Greenwich, CN.

Wood, J. (2000) 'The irrational side of managerial decision-making', *IMD Perspective for Managers*, 7: 1–4.

# Index

Note: Case examples are indicated by **emboldened page numbers**, and Introduction text by roman numerals